All About Bicycle Racing

By

The Editors of Bike World Magazine

Published by

World Publications

BIKE BOOK QUARTERLY NO. 3
February 1975

Library of Congress Catalog Card Number: 74-16791

ISBN: 0-89037-047-8

WORLD PUBLICATIONS, P.O. Box 366, Mountain View, CA 94040

CONTENTS

1

Racer's Starting Guide

Besides the obviously pressing matter of a disclaimer—*All About Bicycle Racing* is an embarrassingly presumptious title—we think there's something in this booklet for everybody.

A great deal of information about bike racing is available to anyone who cares to look for it. The specialty magazines supply all the news anyone could wish for, and *Bike World* carries technical and training feature material plus stories on top US and European races. Books on bike racing are sold by mail order from ads in the magazines, and schedules of upcoming races can be found by contacting your Amateur Bicycle League rep (write Box 669, Wall St. Station, New York, N.Y. 10005 for name and address of your local rep).

What we hope to have done with *All About Bicycle Racing* is to make a contribution of information to American cycle sport that isn't too easily available. We're going to spend very little time on basics that you can find for yourself in the English books—most notably Peter Ward's fine *King of Sports*—and devote the rest of the booklet to articles which may be of use to you in improving your personal best performances on the road or track. If you're a beginner we think you'll find *All About Bicycle Racing* very interesting reading, although there's much that you should probably make an effort to learn elsewhere: how to patch a sewup tire, for instance, or practical skills like following a wheel, which can be best learned by training with more experienced riders.

If you've never raced and are curious, for any of the innumerable reasons that attract people to the sport, this description of the categories of cycle racing is intended for you.

Cycle racing is done on the roads, on indoor or outdoor banked tracks, and on cross-country courses with natural and man-made obstacles which must be cleared by running with the bike on one's shoulder. It used to be the case the one picked a specialty and seldom changed. If you were heavily-muscled the cliche was that you had the build of a sprinter. To some extent this prejudice has been borne out by findings in modern sports medicine, which indicate that the sprinter-type has a greater proportion of what physiologists call "fast-twitch" muscle fibers, while the endurance athlete has more "slow-twitch" muscle. In general, though, no athlete is condemned by heredity to compete only at a predestined distance. In professional bike racing in Europe we find pure roadmen like Eddy Merckx competing in the lucrative winter six-day races, though because it interferes with a road rider's yearly training and racing schedule this is rare.

In the late '40s and throughout the '50s athletes in many sports caught the "bug" of interval training, which had been discovered in Germany and promoted by physiologist Professor Reindell and the running training groups of Gerschler and Stampfl. The concept of the "pure sprinter" was given a further boost by this method which carefully prescribed widely differing training routines for short and long distance athletes.

Interval training's most avid supporters, the Germans, have gradually done a slow modification and even reversal of their official recommendations over the past 10 years or so, realizing that top competitive results just have not appeared as expected when their system was applied to its fullest extent. Endurance, trained for by miles, miles and more miles at a comfortable but not sluggish pace, is now recognized as the foundation of both sprinting and short or long road racing success. As professional track and road cyclist Tim Mountford points out, the essential factor in any event is basic physical fitness.

You don't have to resign yourself to competing only on the road or track because of what you imagine to be your physical "type." California's 1974 state road champion, Lindsay Crawford, is 6'3" and weighs 180 pounds. "Ah well," I hear experienced voices say, "he doesn't do so well on the hills, does he?" It's undeniably true that a heavy rider expends more energy going up hills and descends faster than a light one, but even here generalities are ill-advised. Lindsay won the '74 Tour of Marin, a stage race involving a very tough menu of hill-climbing. Lindsay admits he usually starts the hills ahead and goes over the top at the back of the group, but things tend to equal out in stage races, where endurance is once again the advantage.

Europe's classic bike races are often contested between cyclists of different basic abilities. A "road sprinter"—a roadman with good sprint ability—may have the sting pulled from his strong finishing sprint by a less spectacular rider with unusual hard time trialing ability. A slightly-build Spaniard, famous for his climbing ability, builds a lead in the early hills of a stage race that he hopes his opponents will be unable to whittle away as he loses ground on the later flat sections.

There's plenty of room for the non-muscle-bound on the track, too. Track racing can be one of the most entertaining sidelines for a roadman. If he hasn't got the fast-twitch body composition needed for peak-class results in sprinting, he can choose the 1000-meter time trial, 4000-meter pursuit, or 10-mile massed start.

The 1000-meter time trial has all the physical pleasures of several sprints raced end-to-end, only there's no one's wind shadow to hide in and no tactical considerations beyond the decision of how you'll pace yourself. World championship riders cover the distance in under a minute and 10 seconds, which averages out to over 32 mph.

The sprint is run over a total distance of 1000 meters, too, but times are recorded for only the last 200 meters. The first 800 meters are usually ridden slowly, neither rider wanting to take the front and lose sight of a maneuvering opponent. Lightning fast reactions, tactical experience and intuition, and accelerating

Bike racing's greatest event, the Tour de France. The physical demands of this 23-day, 3000-mile race are rarely encountered in any other sport. (Presse Sports)

strength are needed. If you want to be a sprinter, your best bet is to contact an experienced rider who can teach you tactics, point out your errors, and give you training advice. The same is true of all cycle racing events, of course, but in sprinting the difference is often measured in hundreths of a second and details of riding position, style and tactics which are visible only to experienced eyes become vitally important.

The 4000-meter pursuit (professionals race at 5,000 meters) is started with riders on opposite sides of the track. The idea is to either catch the other rider, in which case you've won the event, or to beat him to the 4000-meter mark. Electronic lap times are now given for each rider at some tracks, making it easier for the rider to judge his position and provoking spectator interest. The riders also check each other frequently at the half-lap and other points.

Pursuiting and team pursuiting, with four riders sharing the lead, are unquestionably the most exciting spectator events in track racing, and put high demands on the rider's pace judgment, endurance and mental collectedness.

Motor-paced racing is done behind the wind shelter of specially designed motorcycles. Speeds go as high as 60 mph. Motor pacing is popular on European indoor tracks but there's practically no such racing done in this country. Riding behind a motorcycle is also a long-established training method for developing the ability to hold a high, steady rate of exertion over long periods, and it's used by riders from both road and track. Professional motor-paced rider Wally Summers gives his advice on this kind of training in an article in this booklet. Incidentally, Wally warns that it is absolutely essential for safety that the pacing motorcycle be equipped with the customary roller for safety. See his article for further details.

Track massed-start distance racing is done in the US at five, 10 or 20 miles. Higher speeds attained on unbraked lightweight fixed-gear track bicycles, the banked track and consequent tactical and bike handling adjustments make it a nervy variant of distance racing.

Road time trials are held at all imaginable distances, depending often on the convenient road courses locally available. Open road racing was banned for years in Great Britain and time trialing became the racers' answer. The standard distances are now 10, 25, 50 and 100 miles, 12 hours and 24 hours. By far the most common distance is 25 miles. To "break the hour" is considered one's badge of entry into the ranks of top-class time trialing. English baker Alf Enger's 25-mile record is 51 minutes flat, or 29.41 mph. The 24-hour time trial record is 508 miles, for an average of 21.2 mph. Time trial courses usually have the finish as close to the start as possible to equalize conditions of wind and slope and make times as comparable as possible between courses. Team time trials with four men sharing the lead are held at the Olympic Games and World Championships, at 100 kilometers.

Road racing is done at any distance over which the human body can be expected to perform and with any weather, road surface or traffic conditions in which the human body can be expected to be mortally imperiled. In Belgium, they race in the rain at night with the populations of whole towns out to cheer. The Tour de France, the world's most famous and gruelling bicycle race, runs over a different route every year on a course roughly circling the outer boundaries of France for about 3000 miles and winding up after 23 days in Paris. The Tour de France caravan consists of approximately 1200 people, and the director of the Tour has absolute authority to divert traffic wherever the race meanders. Millions watch it from roadside, and hundreds of millions see at least part of it throughout most of the world on TV.

Before going into other aspects of road racing, let's dwell on the Tour de France for awhile. The Tour is not an otherwise boring event which has been ballyhooed into a spectator attraction by advertising interests. Until quite recently there were no trade teams, and riders were chosen to represent the land of their origin. Not all sports heroes earn their reputations the way the heroes of the Tour do. The average racing cyclist who's done well as an amateur and has secured a job on a professional team counts himself lucky to even finish the

Tour de France, far less place highly in his first year of this pinnacle of endurance challenges. The 1970 Tour had 27 full road stages and short time trials, covering 2750 miles in 23 days without a rest day. Few vacationing cycletourists average 119.6 miles per day even on flat ground, whereas the Tourmen, under constant racing pressure, have to digest thousands and thousands of feet of climbing in the Alps and Pyrenees. The pure physical demands of the Tour de France capture the attention of people all over the world, and ensure that any cyclist who finishes the race even several hours down on the leaders is an extremely unusual human being.

Road racing has a certain epic quality, and all the road races ever held are wrapped up in the Tour. Marathon running has its Boston, soccer its World Cup, long distance skiing its Vasaloppet. These are the festivals where only the finest of a sport is displayed, where to win and set records is to be unquestionably among the fittest human beings on the face of the earth. The epic side of any road race is traceable to this aspect of celebrating human fitness—to do well you absolutely must give your best (unless you're racing out of your class).

People are rarely challenged to give their physical and mental best in ordinary life nowadays. Pride of work has been swallowed by the machine, the assembly line, the paper shuffling routine. The automobile and electric motor have replaced muscles. But the great renaissance of bicycle road racing has occurred because people inherently need to stretch—to extend their abilities to the limit, to flex and grow. For all the joking that goes on at the starting line, there's always that hush of silence just before the gun, a ritual solemnity that people only "do" spontaneously when something very meaningful is about to happen—a gathering of forces before a great effort, an uncertainness and sudden humility before the unknown outcome. This is to feel one's existence keenly. Pity the poor spectator—he only gets it second-hand.

Bicycle racing is democratic. There's a prize for everybody—not the expensive bike frames and tubular tires that go to the stars who're intent on picking up a big season's prize list, but the pride that, "I may not go as fast as those guys, but anybody who's my physical equal is going to have to work his tail off to beat me!" Or, in the endurance challenges, "I finished—you can blow holes in your precious prize sewups and melt down your trophies, but nobody can take that prize away from me!"

There's constant and uniform complaining among top-level racing cyclists that there's not enough competition in this country. "Bring foreign cyclists and it'll improve the level of racing over here," they tell racing officials at every available opportunity. "Send us to Europe so we can learn to race faster." You'd think, if the ultimate experience in sports was winning, that these fellows would have the best possible situation all sewed-up. They're national champions, they win consistently, and yet they're dissatisfied. Why? It's because they want to stretch, to improve, to be challenged, to be more alive.

At one time there was an elitist pecking order snobbery in bike racing. "If you don't finish in the money, you're nothing!" This attitude, fortunately, is dying among all but a few insecure newcomers. In one sense Vince Lombardi was right—"Winning *is* everything." Complacency is terribly boring; but each person must define for himself realistically just what winning means. We believe racing on a bicycle is a fine instrument on which to call your own unique tune.

THE RACING BICYCLE

BY JOE KOSSACK

Joe Kossack is Technical Editor of Bike World magazine, and Racing Director of a small sponsored ABL of A club. He says he'd still rather ride a bike than write about it.

Stories of the "unknown kid who came out of nowhere and won the (you fill-in the major race name) wearing cut off jeans, a T-shirt and tennis shoes and using an old clunker bike with clinch-on tires" are staples of American cycling lore. Such prodigies can pop up, and may have occurred enough times to give substance to the legend a few years ago when bike racing was at its lowest ebb of interest in the US. Given the low level of training then current, the odd and mismatched equipment everyone used and the fact which we all tend to gloss-over these days, that there was a period when American bike racing did not attract people of top athletic capabilities, an ill-equipped novice wonder could show up at a starting line, and by simple physical superiority wipe out what passed for racers then. It didn't happen often, but it did happen. Perhaps it was to avoid such ego damage that the ABL of A decided not to allow prospective racers to sign up for the first time right at the start of a race.

However, the days of such cycling miracles seem over. American racing has grown up, or rather grown back up, once again attracting athletes who might make their marks in many other sports, but chose bike racing. Standards of training have improved to the point where following the training schedule of one of our top "amateurs" is a full-time job, and the "battle of material" is now waged with frequent costly changes in the latest equipment. Americans are beginning to make their mark in world-class competition. The dam hasn't broken yet, but the US now has a large reserve of well-equipped and better trained Juniors and young Seniors, who if they stay with the sport, promise a floodtide of American World and Olympic medals.

To fit into that class of competition you must become a total racer: a competitor whose preparation is complete and balanced physically, mentally and materially. Luck and sheer native physical ability will always be able to score a few wins, but as US racing becomes more sophisticated the story of the ill-equipped "natural" who beats the fancy racers is going to really become a myth.

There is no magic formula. No table of racing proportions says that starting with good physical conditioning, success is the result of 60% training, 20% tactics, 10% mental attitude and 10% equipment. I believe that these are roughly the correct percentages, but they will of course vary individually and they are all based upon a good state of health and physique.

My recipe for the complete racer lists equipment—what you wear and what you race on—at only 10% of the necessary ingredients. However, that refers to differences between *reasonable* material and equipment, not the possible droll chance of winning a bike race wearing a suit of armor and pushing a wheelbarrow. Don't become an "equipment freak," wasting time and money chasing after the latest of what Fast Eddy or your own cycling hero is using now, and do not disregard the difference which having the right components and right gear for a race might make. Ten percent isn't much, but among well-matched racers, it can put you so far back down the road as to be out of sight. Equipment can't win races, but it can certainly lose them.

PERSONAL EQUIPMENT

The American public still has its doubts about bike racing. The sport has made great progress in recent years toward public acceptance as a "serious" competitive sport. One source of that growing acknowledgement and interest in bike racing by sports fans, prospective sponsors and possible racers is the attitude the racers themselves take to what they do. I believe racing and training in clean, well turned-out clothing and equipment is an aid to performance, both in terms of morale and efficiency, for the racer.

Even if you don't agree it helps your speed, appearing at the start lines and being seen in training looking reasonably neat, clean and, if you will, "professional" is something you owe to the sport itself. There is nothing wrong with a raffish image, but what may seem harmlessly casual to your fellow racers tends to look merely slovenly and dirty to outsiders. Remember, we need a public, we need the sponsors' money, and if we're to come out of the cycling backwoods we need to attract the physically qualified athletes who are now wasting themselves on trivialities like football or baseball.

You are not only what you eat, as the old saw has it, you are what you wear. One step toward becoming a bike racer is looking like one. The clothing and personal equipment used in racing have evolved and reached their present development through years of intensive trials. Some items of personal racing gear may look merely flamboyant, and even downright silly, but their use will soon prove them practical and necessary. While I will make some reference to brand names, bear in mind that in these personal items proper fit is far more important than proper names. Indeed, it is in cycling clothing where sizes and manufacturing standards vary the widest, not only between suppliers of various national origins, but within the different makers' own production.

SHOES

There are shoes for cyclo-touring and there are shoes for bike racing, and the two types are not the same. A suitable racing shoe isn't designed for walking comfort, and a very small amount of walking in them soon gives you an extra pair of touring shoes. Bike racing shoes of the current "sprint" conformation have the usual light leather uppers, often perforated for ventilation and vanity, no heels, a steel reinforced sole with perhaps further holes originally designed to drain rain water out, and a very high arch to keep the foot in the sprint position.

A current fad is toward soles of double thickness, the result of Fast Eddy's Adidas supplementary contract no doubt, but the added weight and change in saddle position due to the double sole isn't worth the added stiffness. Better designed steel or nylon inner reinforcements as in the new Saba or latest Detto Pietro shoes serve the same purpose of spreading the pedal pressure over a wider portion of the bottom of the foot.

Remember, racing shoes aren't supposed to be comfortable off of the bike. The key is that they must fit your foot like an extra skin, so tightly that your foot cannot slip around inside them under pedalling effort, losing power and risking friction abrasions or blisters. I recommend that you race wearing socks, and that you buy shoes taking at least light cotton socks into account. If track sprinting is your thing, and you can afford more than one pair of racing shoes, then by all means have another pair that fit tight without socks, but for training and road racing socks cut chaffing and absorb annoying perspiration.

There are some racing shoes being now marketed, including a model being sold under the Cinelli name, that are supplied with shoe cleats already mounted, allowing slight or even no adjustments. Unless you are quite sure these anonymous Italian craftsmen had your foot in mind, buy shoes that let you mount the cleats exactly where *you* will need them.

There are a number of formulas for locating the proper cleat position. The tried and true one is designed to put the cleat slot right under the ball of your foot when the cleat locks into the rear pedal edge. Providing you are starting with the correct toeclip length, put in a few miles wearing the shoes without the cleats until a definite rear pedal edge line appears on the shoe sole. Then mount the cleat so that the slot is about 1/16" back of this line. The offset keeps a tiny gap between the toeclip and your shoe toe, but is sometimes omitted to get just the right position. It is important to keep the cleat slot "square" with the pedals, unless some physical problems require you to pedal either toe-in or toe-out.

TA makes the best line of metal cleats, and if you have a good stiffener inside your shoe you shouldn't need the added weight of a long-based cleat like the TA No. 38 road pattern. I strongly suggest that you or your shoemaker use heftier brads than those supplied, or even a few rivets. Providing you do stay off your racing shoes for all but riding, plastic or leather cleats are durable enough. The light French "Aero" plastic cleat is popular again, and a number of US leather craftsmen are making neat custom leather ones.

Sizing racing shoes is a problem. All but the English handmade Reynolds and Salisbury shoes are marked in metric sizes, but there is little uniformity between what the French Hungaria, the Belgian Hector Martin, the Spanish Ribo, the Italian Crodoni, or any of the others mean by a given metric-numbered size. Unless you are absolutely sure of where you fit in a manufacturer's sizing scheme don't buy cycling shoes mail order. It seems all the continental racing shoes come in one width: too narrow. I suppose it's to promote tight fit and allow using narrow pedals with good clearance, but if you must have a wider racing shoe, and if you can find any, Hector Martin used to make them.

SHORTS

Here brand name means nothing, but if you must deal by mail Sergal, Seghezzi, Alex-Sport, Lutz, Emily K, Unis-Sport and Du Rocher usually turn out a fair product, Since you are again dealing with a size problem, and with widely varying standards of quality for the most important part of cycling shorts—the chamois insert—if you can, see it before you buy it.

Look for a thick and fuzzy (to start with) chamois seat; one without obvious thin spots or evidence that the cow lost an argument to a barbed-wire fence. The best design for the chamois seems to be built up of three pieces with laid-over jointing seams, and reinforced with a number of sewn-through circular seams.

I prefer the shorts themselves to be at least part wool; the all-wool type both seems to be pricing itself out of the market, and lately of low quality, too stretchy and loosely woven. However, the benefits of wool are well known: warming when it's cool, and absorbent without clamminess when it's warm. Spun nylon shorts of Helenca or Bri-Nylon are available. They are lighter, cooler and less expensive, but do not keep you warm enough, nor can they dispose of perspiration as can wool or shorts with a fair amount of wool in their fabric. Though there are cotton racing shorts marketed the most expensive part of a pair of shorts is still the chamois, and the minor savings in price for the cotton body isn't worth the rapid wear.

The first thing a novice racer objects to in his cycling shorts is the leg length. If they fit correctly they should extend to mid-thigh or a bit below. This isn't a fashionable or even a visually pleasing length with most physiques. The answer is that this length has been worked out over the years to afford the least chance of the legs of the shorts riding or rucking-up between the legs and causing chaffing, without having the shorts so tight at the upper leg as to interfere with circulation. It's not sporty looking and it will cut your sun tan, but resist the impulse to shorten the legs past mid-thigh level. Shorts are available in different lengths, with "road" designated types having longer legs than those marked "track," and shorts identified as having "Belgian" lengths being the longest. "Madison" style shorts for track use are supposed to have higher and reinforced backs as well as a special pocket for the "jamming tool."

It is of utmost importance that your racing shorts be kept scrupulously clean to avoid infection of the minor skin abrasions and irritations that always result from hard training and racing. They must be clean of any soiling and of any chemicals that your skin might become sensitive to, and it appears to be easier to get the chamois and shorts clean than to keep them chemically neutral. Any washing with water shortens the life of the chamois. So far water seems to be the only way to wash out the other cleaning substances, but it's my belief it should be used only as a rinse. I recommend regular dry cleaning for shorts, with several plain water rinses afterwards, hand shaping the chamois to pull out wrinkles and air drying at room temperature. Under racing conditions substitute a thorough soaking and light kneading in rubbing alcohol for the dry cleaning, but remember that a water rinse is required.

Traditional methods are handwashing with a mild soap (not a detergent) in lukewarm water, with many rinses, hand shaping and air drying. I do not think cold water soaps of the Woolite type get sufficient infection-promoting dirt out for long run use, but they are better than nothing.

JERSEYS

Those of you who follow every bit of advice in the rest of this booklet will soon be wearing national or even world championship jerseys, or perhaps those supplied by your professional sponsor, but until that happens, and for the rest of us compelled to choose and pay for our own jerseys there are a few things to watch for.

Here again there are metric sizes as well as English/American ones, but the European cycling nations and the various makers have done a far better job of standardization, allowing some reasonable hope that a mail-order-picked size will fit.

British/US chest size in inches	French & Italian metric size	Belgian metric size
30"	1	—
32"	2	0
34"	3	1
36"	4	2
38"	5	3
40"	6	4
42"	7	5
44"	8	6

Jerseys for track racing have no pockets, and are designed to fit very tightly. For track streamlining is most important, and closer-woven materials are used than in road jerseys to lessen any wind drag, even though it may cause more sweating.

True road jerseys have a number of pockets at the chest as well as some on the lower back. In the old days these were for stowing one's own spare tires, food and tools as the rules required of each racer in those Spartan times. Of course, modern practice except in some rare racing instances does not require the racer to pack it all himself, allowing wheel changes, aid in repairs and food and drink to be handed up. So smaller and fewer pockets are now the stylish thing in road jerseys, with the type with pockets only on the lower back, formerly known as a "time trial jersey" gaining in general road use.

All jerseys should have a zipper at the neck, and elasticized knit collar and cuffs. If you do race with a jersey having front pockets, they should either be kept empty or fitted with buttons to prevent them from catching the wind. While a long-sleeved road jersey is nice to have as an extra, separate arm warmers are more useful.

Wool or part-wool again is the best material for jerseys, for all of the same reasons: warmth, and especially wool's unique ability to breathe with you, providing the right balance of cooling ventilation and protection.

However, there are now very good completely artificial fabric jerseys available offered by makers who are too numerous to list and which are made of cotton in combination with a man-made yarn, and I feel the English Lutz jersey of that type to be the best hot weather one on the market. Once again, avoid those that are too closely woven for anything except short track events; and no all-nylon jersey has been found suitable for road use yet.

A jersey should fit fairly tightly without binding under the arms when you're on the handlebar "drops," and be sure that it is cut long enough to cover the small of the back when you lean into the bars.

Washing, especially with the man-made and cotton fiber jerseys, can be in hotter water than required for chamois shorts, but harsh detergents still should be avoided, and rinsing all the cleaning material out after the washing must be done with care. Of course, wool and part wool jerseys should be treated in the same manner as your shorts, with special attention to avoid shrinking.

HELMETS

The traditional "crash hat," as the British call it, is a number of leather or leatherlike padded tubes arranged in positions that years of cycling experience have shown afforded a reasonable amount of head protection in exchange for a reasonable amount of weight. These helmets are made in Europe, Mexico and Japan; though cycling legend is that the type was invented in the US before the turn of the century, there is no active American maker now. Sizings vary between manufacturers, and there are too many actual makers and proprietary brand names to list. Those sold under the Cinelli and Detto Pietro marques and those made by Alisian in England maintain high standards.

The heaviest of the traditional patterns, with extra padding, and added protection for the forehead and around the ears, are generally designated as "track," "piste," or "madison" types, while road versions are built lighter and are designed to sit higher on the head. The difference in weight between the types isn't great, and the track style offers a lot more protection in every sort of use—touring, training and road and track racing. However, here again fad is king, and every cycling novice has the mental image of himself looking like a debonair continental pro—with a tiny, light road helmet perched rakishly high on the side of the head.

A number of full surface helmets are being pushed for racing use. Some like the CCM and Cooper models were originally made for other sports, climbing, hockey, etc. The new Bell version was designed from the ground (head) up for cycling use with racing and touring testing before introduction of their production model. The MSR cycling helmet is a lightened version of their excellent rock climber's hat. I don't believe a verdict can be made yet on these space-age looking affairs. Many of them do seem to offer increased protection against head injuries compared to the old patterns. However, others do not seem well-made, with brittle plastic skins and exposed rivets, and some, those coming from other sports, do not provide the protection for the forehead, ears and especially the back of the head, that can be had in a good track style "crash hat."

OTHER CLOTHING

Track or training suits with long sleeved zippered jackets, and tapered bottoms with ankle zips are handy, and a great ego boost toward making you feel the complete racer. In most climates the standard acrylic or spun-nylon types are not warm enough by themselves for cold weather training, and should be used over a number of layers of undershirts and jerseys, and even tights. These outfits are really meant for turning a few warm-up or cool-down miles on the race day, and for use between events, showing the club or pro sponsor's "colors."

Off-season training can be eased with heavier weight training trousers or knickers having their own sewn-in chamois seat. Separate arm and leg warmers give good value and good protection. They don't cost much—far, far less than a training suit—and can be home-made with minimal skills from worn long sleeved tops and tights. Be sure not to use too tight an elastic so as to interfere with circulation.

Gloves or mitts ought to be as compulsory as helmets. They are excellent protection at a small burden of weight and cost. While hard leather mitts last longer, and those with padded palms ease road shock, the lighter chamois or suede Spanish made track mitts seem to cause fewer blisters, and cost less than the others.

THE RACING BICYCLE

Traveling by Bike, the first booklet of this series, received a favorable review in *Cycletouring,* the magazine of the Cyclists' Touring Club of Britain. The review put words to a feeling I last heard from French national track coach Louis (Toto) Gerardin: "It is no bad thing, but American writers do seem—in a style somewhat amusing to most . . . to dissect and analyse their subjects in a very comprehensive and clinical way." Perhaps so. However, perhaps this attention to details and close consideration of all the variables may speed our progress toward racing success, and perhaps a willingness to learn from the experiences of others will get us there faster.

When it comes to racing bikes and their components it is possible, and even pleasant, to lose sight of the goal—the winning of races—and become totally taken up in the gadget aspects of biking. This is as wrong as ignoring the technology of the sport, and a far too common fault of the US bikie.

Ounces and inches may indeed make a difference, but only as part of the total preparation of the complete and competent racer. The best or most expensive equipment in the world will never make up for deficiencies in training, tactics or mental approach. These categories of preparation, which can be gained only through time and effort, never just by money, are all far more important than fractional advantages in equipment weight and performance. Know your bike, learn to select the best equipment for you and your sort of racing, and then learn how to use and maintain it for optimum results; but always remember it is the racer, not the machinery that counts the most. That's Merckx's name in the record books, not Campagnolo's.

There is a great deal of first rate equipment on the market these days. Back in the bad old days of post-WW II US racing everyone used mis-matched and oddball bikes and components, because there were no American makers and European goods were scarce. After a period of experimentation US bike racing then settled down for a long period where everyone who was anyone in the sport used nothing but Campagnolo equipment. They were indeed the best components available in nearly every class of component. Things are changing now. Campagnolo material is still at the top in most categories—those having to do with performance as well as price—but in nearly every class of goods adequately functioning, more readily available, and somewhat lower priced components are now offered by other makers. French, Japanese and even some American goodies compete for the racer's favor, stimulating Campagnolo as well toward more rational pricing and further design improvements.

While the US racer can't go far wrong using a full set of Campy topline components, for those who do not wish to pay quite so much monetary tribute to the Wizards of Vicenza, and who are interested in other, perhaps equally successful, design approaches, a wide range of choices are available. In a survey such as this they can only be outlined, and the chief emphasis will be put on what is now popular with the racing community, not the vast assortment of what is now available in components and equipment.

Of course, one quick way around the whole problem is to simply go to a trustworthy shop, and after letting its staff get to know your racing level and ambitions, buy "off the peg" the bike they recommend, with the changes in detailed specifications they think you ought to use. If it's a shop owned or staffed by people involved in the US bike racing scene, you might find yourself set-up to match their cycling ideals, not mine, but it's doubtful you'll be steered far wrong.

As a general rule you will find that the racing model bikes imported into the US from European manufacturers involved in professional sponsorship arrangements in Europe make the best buys "off the dealer's shelves," needing only minor modifications to fit your own style and physique. These are not always the most handsome looking machines, and it is quite possible that the topline Gitane, Motobecane, Colnago, Bianchi or even Raleigh sent to America isn't an exact duplicate of the ones supplied to that pro team's big-name racers, or even made by the same people. However, the best bikes imported under the marques of makers now connected with professional racing are usually designed and equipped in keeping with current racing practices and ideas. Topline Peugeots have always been excellent value for money. Their finish isn't outstanding, and the maker's insistence on mostly French components sometimes means quality is compromised, but it's a real racing machine at prices half those of other more Italianate offerings.

FRAMES

The non-steel frameset is making its way into racing. The successes of the Polish racers at the Montreal World's revived interest in their Italian-made screwed-and-glued aluminum framesets, ignored for many years by the racing experts. There are at least three titanium frames in current production, and they have had racing successes, and enjoy a strong following among US racers. There are three US firms experimenting with prototypes or early production models of carbon fiber frames, and one is supposed to be entrusted to John Howard for real racing use. Perhaps the next edition will provide details of this new non-ferrous cycling wave of the future, or perhaps it will all have blown away as another fad by then.

I certainly think the titanium frame has a place in racing, both for road and light track use, and will survive their presently too-high prices. I expect the fad for aluminum frames to pass, and expect to hear different opinions of their liveliness after their owners have raced them a tough season's worth; but at the present price the aluminum frameset is a good bargain, and if not punished with hard racing ought to give adequate service and a pleasant ride. The carbon or graphite fiber bikes are still too new to judge.

Therefore, most serious racing is still done on steel, and this survey will keep to the conventional steel frame.

Racing framesets are made from butted steel tubesets. The butting refers to internal thickening of the tubes at their points of juncture at the corners of the frame, in this manner gaining strength and spreading stress loads without undue weight. The big names in butted tube sets are Reynolds, Columbus, Vitus, Tange and Ishiwata. The sets are supplied in different gauges or weights with the heaviest designed for use with sprint or six-day type track frames, a more or less standard mid-weight type for road racing and some track bikes, and extra light tubesets meant for track pursuit or road time trial bikes.

The tubesets are usually mounted in metal sleeves called "lugs," and respected names are Prugnat, Nervex and Bocama. Low temperature bronze brazing or even lower temperature silver soldering is used to put it all together.

Track frames have far more upright angles than those used on road bikes, with 75° head and seatmast angles not being too unusual these days. Rear triangles are short and beefy, 16" or so, and thick stays are used for sprinters' machines. Track forkrakes are in the neighborhood of an inch or so, and the total wheelbase can be around 38". All this makes for a nervous and responsive mount, without any concessions to comfort. True six-day track frames are built a bit easier, and there are other variations for specialized pursuit frames. All track frames are made with rearward-opening back forkends, and usually have higher bottom brackets than used for road racers to accommodate to the track bankings.

While there are many specialized designs for road frames matching certain types of racing such as time trial work, and even certain events like the classic Paris-Roubaix race which are held on the worst roads possible, two standardized road types have evolved: criterium bikes and stage race bikes. The criterium-oriented design is for short, fast racing, with a premium put on alert bike handling through many turns. The stage race design is usually a longer-wheelbased bike directed more toward stability.

Most US racing is of the criterium sort, and it is the extreme lines of the criterium frameset that form the American bikie's idea of what a bike should look like. As our racing becomes more sophisticated and more stage races and distance events are scheduled, the racing community is going to be forced to re-think its ideas about frame design and component choices.

The typical criterium design is, as has been often noted, something like a track bike with road forkends. built "square" or under "square" for most frame sizes (that is, with toptube the same length or less than the seat mast) and having 73°-74° head and seat angles; rear triangles of 16¾" or fractionally less (the absolute minimum for derailleur operation), short fork rakes, and wheelbases around 39".

A true criterium-designed frame should have a higher bottom bracket than an equivalent stage race or general purpose frame to allow pedalling through corners and taking the closest line possible. This is something to watch for; since stock lugs can only be distorted so far, frame makers sometimes get the extreme head angles desired by their customers by simply lowering bottom bracket height below even the normal 10½". Italian bikes, even with prestigious names, often have this design aberration.

Standard road racing frame designs of the stage race or general purpose type are built more "open," with slightly longer toptubes, slightly slacker angles of 72°-73°, more forkrake, and longer rear triangles. All this results in a longer wheelbase—making for a less responsive feel, but with sufficient comfort for long, long miles of racing without pointless road shock and strain. These design differences seem quite small, almost trivial, but they are important. Even short rides on differing frames demonstrate what large effects such minor-seeming changes may cause.

In a reoccurrence of another old fad, frames meant for six-plate rear blocks are again coming from Europe. The rear axle width of such bikes must be wider, making it difficult to get proper spacing with standard-width hubs. However, if enough people follow this fad for 12-speed bikes, all the problems will be transferred to the 10-speed diehards. That is far from happening as yet, and I recommend sticking to a standard 10-speed setup.

CRANKSETS

Dural, cotterless cranksets are the racer's choice for road and track. Crank lengths were standardized after years of experimentation at 165mm for track and 170mm for road use. However, America raises big boys, and current theory tends toward pushing big gears rather than twiddling small ones, so longer crank lengths are gaining more favor. Merckx and other continental superstars have raced on 175mm and on 177.5's, but even for our milkfed powerhouses 172.50mm length cranks are the maximum advisable road racing size. The longer ones inhibit your sprint and seem to take an awful lot out of you. It is still my opinion, and current European practice, that the acceleration/deceleration pattern of criterium racing, imposed by many corners and close maneuvers, favors 170mm or even 167.50mm cranks.

In keeping with our trends toward giantism many US trackies have gone from 165mm length to 167.50 or 170's. French star Daniel Morelon often sprints on 167.50's, but Nicholson and other pro trackies who are also big boys are more often observed using 165's. That may be because their riding style is tailored for the small, steeply banked indoor tracks of the six-day scene. When and if America gets any small, modern-designed tracks built, we will probably see a strong return to shorter track lengths; they can be sprinted better, and don't trip you on the bankings.

Campagnolo's "Nuovo Record" road model and "Record" track model cranksets are still the current standards of excellence, with fine bearings and minimum crankarm and chainwheel flex. Their new "Super Record" road and track models employ mostly interchangeable lighter components at vastly increased prices. Sugino's "Mighty-Compe" and "Custom-Compe" cranksets have complete interchangeability of parts with Campagnolo's. Use of their chainwheels on Campy arms can be a money saver, but on the whole neither the steel nor dural portions are first quality.

Shimano's "Dura-Ace" set is interchangeable with Campy except for the right crankarm and chainwheels, which go down to 39T instead of 42T. The arms are slightly more flexy than Campy's, and be sure to get their optional type 75S chainwheels—made out of a denser material than their standard 14S types.

Zeus "Criterium" sets are popular in Europe, and seem to give fair value for money. The makers have announced a new super "2000" series crankset along the lines of Campy's "Super Record," but it hasn't reached the market yet.

French-made Stronglight types 93 and 99 and TA "Professional" three-pin sets are less costly, and offer good racing performance, but just do not have the Campy or Campy-like cachet required to attract fad-motivated American racers.

Current road practice starts with chainwheel combinations of 52T and 42T—far wider jumps than used to be recommended for racing. Very useful combinations under current theories can be made with a 53-44 or 45 setup, and some of the Merckx-inspired big gear pushers like to think they can handle a 56-48 combination.

Derailleur-sized 3/32" chain is becoming more popular for track use, but 1/8" chain and chainwheels are still used by the majority of trackies, and do seem to provide a bit of extra stiffness. Good track combinations can be built starting with front chainwheels from 47T to 50T, with an old theory favoring the use of gears making bigger circles front and rear for a given ratio as being smoother operating.

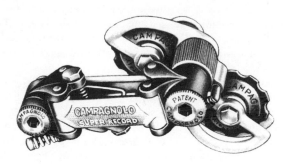

DERAILLEURS

Racing derailleur sets don't have the tourist's problems of spanning wide gearing jumps from 13T or 14T to 30+ rears, and of winding-up all the chain needed for wide ratios. Even for the big gear pushers and even for mountain racing, rear sprockets don't often get above 24T, with a bottom of 21T on the rear being most common. What racing derailleurs have to be is quick and positive, and most of the equipment now marketed meets that need.

At present the best choices are Campagnolo's "Nuovo Record," Huret's "Jubilee" (Model 2240—for Campy style forkends) and the Sun Tour "Cyclone." The Campagnolo costs the most, but it's still the best on average. The Huret is the lightest, but has a bit of lag in the rear unit, and works better with downtube levers having smaller drums than Huret's own. The "Cyclone" is the least expensive, but seems to wear the fastest, and its front shifter will distort with too vigorous use.

The next best units, and with derailleurs the groupings are all close, are the Shimano "Dura-Ace" and Simplex "Super L-J" sets.

Downtube shift levers have less lag than handlebar end controls. On the continent, where they are perhaps less gentlemanly about such things or take their racing ultra-seriously, handlebar end controls are not often used. There is a well-founded fear that during a finishing sprint the racer next to you might reach out and shift you into a gear you don't want.

FREEWHEELS

Splined freewheels where the plates may be changed without pulling the entire unit off the hub, and where a minimum number of extra cogs will make up a maximum number of ratios, should be the racer's choice. High-priced examples of the type are the alloy cogged Maillard "700s" and Sun Tour "Winners" or the part-titanium Zeus "2000's"; these have shorter useful lives than steel plate models, and might be best saved for ultra-important events. Maillard makes a steel kit version with extra plates, and the Cyclo-Pans kit is still the best bet for general racing and training use.

WHEELS

Current road racing practice favors low flange quick release hubs. If well maintained, the cup and cone bearing Campagnolo "Record" and Shimano "Dura-Ace" function better than any other makes, with the Zeus only tiny fractions less smooth. Shielded or sealed bearing hubs will give you longer periods of good operation under adverse weather and maintenance conditions, but do not equal freshly lubed and adjusted firstline cup and cone types. Trackies still prefer the added stiffness of high flange hubs, and all it will take to bring them back to general road use would be their adoption by the next European superstar.

While the leading men of continental pro teams are supplied with wheels in special combinations running down to the 18-spoke, two-cross wheels recently used (unsuccessfully) in the Grand Prix des Nations road time trial, most racing, road and track, is still done, and won, on wheels spoked 36 x 36, three-cross, and that is what I recommend for general use. Wash-plated spokes such as the Robergel "Sport" last longer than equal gauge stainless or chromed types.

Sewup rims range from the ultra light Mavic "gold" "extra Leger" and Super Champion "Medaille d'Or" to models around 420 grams. Something around 340 to 390 grams, depending on your weight, riding style, and roads, is recommended for most road racing. Track rims are usually lighter, but track wheels have a different range of problems involving the loads imposed by sprint jumps and cornering, requiring rather heavy wheels.

Road racing sewups run an enormous range of weights, treads and prices. Without getting caught up in a mass of detail, good racing types run about 220 to 260 grams for good road surfaces, up to 290 for poorer roads, and in general silk-cased tires are more durable and seem to roll out faster than cotton-cased models. Many firms now offer tubulars with casings or "pockets" of mixed composition, part polyester fabric, etc., and so far they seem to equal silks in durability.

There are a great number of tubular brand names, but many Italian makes are made by the same parent company as the Vittoria and D'Allessandro tires, and many French marques like Michelin look a good deal like Wolber's. Prestige names for tubulars are Clement, D'Alessandro, Canetti and Dourdoigne; their models are usually expensive, but provide high quality and racing security. Very useful training, and some specialized racing tires, can be found at lower average prices among makers like Barum, Wolber and Hutchinson.

HANDLEBARS AND STEMS

Trackies sometimes still use steel bars and stems for absolute minimum flex, but everywhere else in racing dural is king for these components. Most road racers and some track-types use wide "Maes" pattern bars of 16" to 17" width, providing sufficient alternate positions for sprinting, climbing and cornering, with the breadth and depth needed for unconstricted breathing. Stems are usually of the allen-keyed type now keeping to an extension range of 95 mm to 115 mm for bikes that fit their riders. Good names for both bars and stems are Cinelli, TTT, Satri (also sold as Mavic) and Nitto.

SADDLES AND SEATPOSTS

Nearly all racing, road and track, is done on plastic-bottomed saddles these days—some on the naked plastic, but more often on the slightly heavier and more costly leather-topped versions or much more costly padded leather-topped models. Unica (same as Cinelli) favors suede-like covers called "chamois" or to maximize price, "buffalo," while the other leading maker, Ideale, likes to think its customers are riding on "glove leather." Arius and YFC produce excellent lower-priced leather-topped plastic saddles, but the two most currently "in" models are the Unica (or Cinelli) No. 3, "Tour de France" and the Ideale "2002."

Some more old-fashioned racers, and those troubled by bottom problems, still use the traditional regular leather saddles—far heavier, but providing more comfort after being broken in. The Brooks "Pro" and Ideale 90 series are the favored of the all-leather types, and even the European superstars will be found using them during long stage races and during periods when, shall we say, their fundaments tell them they are "human, all too human."

Seatposts are usually the dural integrated adjustable models, and either by Campagnolo (Type 1044 standard, Type 1044/a super-light) or one of the many Campy copies, the best of which are by Zeus and S-R. Excellent non-Campy style designs, showing both their makers' and their users' desire for novelty, are offered by Satri and TTT.

BRAKES

Everyone who's anyone in racing, and everybody who wishes to look like someone in racing does it with sidepull brakes. The story is that they provide better control and quicker responses than the centerpull types that were the absolute hallmark of racing not so long ago. That the best of the centerpulls, the Mafac "Competition" or "2000" and Zeus "2000" models, function just as well is merely to confuse the faddies with the facts, and their re-introduction to the racing scene must await the time when a European superstar of the Merckx wattage adopts them (read: "is paid to use them"). Campagnolo started the trend back to sidepulls, and their versions are great looking and work as well as is possible. Less costly sidepulls that function about as smoothly as Campy's are Shimano's "Dura-Ace," Dia-Compe's "Gran-Compe" and perhaps the new Weinmann "Carrera," which is now undergoing testing.

PEDALS

The pick of the racing pedals for road and track are Campagnolo's black alloy Record extra-light types, but the light cages do wear fast with heavy racing usage. There is to be a "Super Record" pedal substituting a titanium pedal axle for added cost at still lower weight. Campy's own chrome steel standard "Record" series pedals rate at the top in everything but the low weight derby, and are my recommendation for racing use.

There are a number of excellent pedals, mostly of the Campy style, now on the market at lesser costs, and at almost equal quality. The Lyotard type 65 is the best with the Zeus, Pro-Ace and MKS models grouped close after, and the Maillard "700" and older Lyotard models in the next ranking.

Bindas are the best, and absolutely stretchless toestraps, and Christophe or Paturaud chrome and GB stainless steel are the best racing toeclips.

PRE-RACE PREPARATION

Before hitting the start line for your first novice race or your Nth National BAR event teach yourself a pre-race routine that starts days before the race. Ritualize your preparation beginning with making sure you'll have your ABL racing license with you, and getting all your spares, racing clothing, water bottles and other necessary gear ready and together well in advance of the race.

Your bike should be checked out before the event. Racing lubrication of all the bearings other than the headset's should be with lighter weight materials than your training practice. All cups and bearings should be adjusted and tried out after adjustments. Check for play in the hubs and bottom bracket and check every bolt, especially those in the crankset, for looseness. Inspect and replace things as inexpensive as brake blocks and cables and as expensive as tubulars, if necessary, or if you have any doubts about them at all. Of course, your wheels should be true, at least at the start of a race, and be sure to check your toestraps and toeclips for tears or cracks. Having a foot pull out is a disheartening way to lose a finishing sprint for the line.

In your personal race preparation you might follow European practice and use an embrocation—a rubbing lotion—to protect and warm up the leg muscles just before the start. Somehow US racers have the idea that doing this sort of massage for themselves or for their fellow racers is demeaning or even unmanly. That's a stupid attitude: the use of prepared embrocations like Musclor or Curacho or homemade witches' brews are a useful racing tradition. A quick pre-race leg rubdown with the bare hands serves to loosen up a friend or clubmate, and might be the sort of thing that adds up to a win.

RACING'S ABL MENTORS

BY VIC BLACK

Vic Black is a 34-year-old mechanical designer who's serving as the 1975 ABL representative for the nation's "busiest" racing area—Northern California. Vic's association with racing is a long one. He's been involved with racing for at least 15 years, and has five full racing seasons behind him. Vic's a member of the Menlo Park, Calif.-based Pedali Alpini club.

I'm a beginning rider. I don't know the first thing about racing. I'm getting in shape and am interested in "taking the first step." How do I find out how to sign up to be a bike racer?

If you're in a district that has organized racing, you can contact somebody who's into the sport and get in touch with your district ABL representative. Cy-

Aces Ball, Neel, Skarin & Howard in pre-race ritual. (Ted Mock)

cling's a club sport, so I think the most important thing would be to get in touch
with a club. You can ask about this in bike shops. If you're in a district that
doesn't have much activity and you don't know where the closest club is, you can
write the ABL national office at P. O. Box 669, Wall St. Station, New York, NY
10005. They'll give you the address and phone number of your local rep. The
most important thing is to get in touch with a club, though, because that's where
most riders get their experience riding with a pack. You'll learn a lot of things
from the other riders.

How complicated is it to sign up?

The thing that's really unfortunate about it is that there's a major outlay
of cash involved. You have to pay to get your registration with the ABL, you
have to have a certain type of equipment that's required for safety, like a helmet;
and you have to have white socks and black shorts for uniformity of appearance
so we can get sponsorship in the sport. We're trying to get around the outlay of
cash by lowering the registration cost as much as we can. Otherwise, it's not
complicated—just get your ABL card and racing gear and come to a race.

What happens when I go to a race for the first time; Do they check everybody's card to make sure you're in the ABL?

Yes. In this district next year (Northern California-Northern Nevada)
we're going to have more stock bike races in conjunction with our sanctioned
events. They'll probably be held before our Twilight Series evening training races, for instance. That way the stock bike racers won't clog up our schedule at
major criteriums, and it'll give stock bike racers a chance to try the sport without
making a major financial commitment.

We also plan to set up procedures and policies for racing so that they're always the same. This way we'll have better officiating. Too many people come

into the sport and are disillusioned after awhile—I'd like to see more of a lifelong involvement. A lot of people come in, pay their money and don't really get what they expect—partly because we're growing so fast that we haven't been able to organize properly. One person can't handle the whole load anymore—I was up until one o'clock this morning doing the ABL paperwork and just realized I'd signed my name over 1500 times this week. Rich Holder, last year's ABL rep for this district, sent out over 5,500 leters—that averages out to over 15 per day without a letup.

When you get right down to it, what happens at a bike race is that a bunch of people show up and go around in circles on their bicycles. So what's the big need for an organization?

There are all kinds of reasons for the complexity, annoying as it sometimes is. Given a complex society, it takes an organization to create an effective interface between racing and the world around: safety, public relations, international team formation and travel involvements all demand organization and control. We have to keep bike racing out of society's way at the same time that we make friends with society. In the past we've had an easy time of driving out in the country, racing, then driving back home. We haven't had any trouble with the small crowds, but now wherever we go bike racing is attracting lots of attention. Until recently the California Highway Patrol was communicating with us through news releases because they didn't know there was a sanctioning body involved. They'd tell us how things were going to be, and we weren't communicating back to them. Big race fields demand a little more control and communication with public officials.

You raised the question yourself—what does a rider get out of the ABL?

The ABL puts in an awful lot of work trying to get the sport before a lot of people and trying to make it easy for riders to compete in a full schedule of racing. There's a newsletter that comes with your membership in the ABL—*Cyclenews*. We have an international fund which pays for most riders' trips to international competition, and the ABL is also working to promote sponsorships for clubs by private businesses; because of sponsorship there's more travel money available to the riders. Most riders travel quite a bit, and the money helps.

If an ABL official tells you to get out of a race because you're doing something wrong, do you have to obey him?

Yes, definitely. In fact, when we talked with the Highway Patrol earlier this year they were amazed that we had such a strict rulebook. One of the rules says we have to adhere to the rules of the road even while racing. As it turns out, we're some of the best-disciplined users of the road. On the Tour of the Sierra when Officer Dean Rupp was worried about being able to stop 80 riders coming down the road, we just told them to stop and they immediately stopped and sat in the ditch waiting for us to work out our differences with the police. They were rather amazed that we could control 80 riders so easily.

If I were to go to a race where the competition is over my head or I just felt like watching for a change, could I help out as a timer or something?

Yes, there are always places where volunteers can help—all you have to do is get in touch with the officials at the race and ask to help out.

2

Without This There's Nothing More

Tim Mountford is the most successful of a scant handful of American racing cyclists who've tried to enter the modern European professional racing scene. Tim barely lost to Leijn Loevesijn in the finals of the 1971 professional sprint championships, and was a popular rider on the six-day tracks. What Tim says here about reaching peak condition and the importance of basic physical fitness applies to all cyclists, from pure sprinter to stage racer. The questions were asked by Bike World editor George Beinhorn.

GB: Would you comment on the relationship between early-season training and achieving a performance peak at the time of the national championships in late summer.

Mountford: Although it wasn't the case when I was a sprinter, now I'm a very firm believer in physical fitness. It's hard for American cyclists to conceive of physical fitness—especially track cyclists—except in the rare case when they've been exposed to it.

Competition is the name of the game—your competition will make you. A person can peak out to a certain level, and erroneously feel he's gone as far as he can. Let's say for example that you've set up your 92-inch gear, or whatever you're going to use for the 4000-meter pursuit, and on a good track like Northbrook you do a five-minute 4000 meters. You believe you're peaked out, but is that realistic? You get a European over here who's peaked out and put him on Northbrook and he'll do a ride in the 4:50s. You're both equal human beings more or less, in strength, but peaking out is relative and a mental thing as well.

Once you start feeling satisfied, you level off and your brain starts telling you, "OK, this is it, this is maximum." You stop achieving. But if there's someone there to tell you, or you go to Europe, and you're faced with seeing people do better than you then you can understand: "Hey, I'm not really peaked out— there's more work involved, more mental stress and strain and psychic energy has to be applied to it." The European rider has these advantages over his American counterpart, and they help him reach a higher peak: enthusiasm, support, the environment, acceptance and exposure.

This is not as true in the case of American sprinters. A fellow like Gibby Hatton and a couple of others will ride 11.2 or 11.1—so the ability is here. But in bicycle racing there are other things involved as well. It's not like the 100-yard dash where a guy just gets in his lane and goes. There's so much mental stress and strain that it plays games with your body and chemical makeup at a time when you go to the line. Sometimes you just don't perform. Basic physical fitness helps prevent this situation.

GB: A lot of people say that if cycling is ever going to be publically supported in this country, it will have to come through track and criterium racing. With something like five new tracks going up now and more track promotions coming, perhaps more road riders will be wanting to ride the track. How do they pick up on a program to start developing the specific abilities to ride the pursuit, the kilometer or the sprints?

Mountford: Well, this relates back again to physical fitness. If you are physically fit you have the legs and the lungs and everything. If you have your basic foundation—to do a 100-kilometer time trial or a 1000-meter time trial, to be a pursuiter or a sprinter—then you can branch off into different areas, but until you have that you're not a bike rider.

I think a sprinter in the first part of the year should forget about the fact that he's a sprinter. He should get in physical condition, *then* in March or April he can go out and ride a 100-kilometer criterium and go with a three- or four-man breakaway in his 52 x 14 gear. When late spring comes he can get on the track and warm up, go through six sprints, do his jumps off the bank, put in an hour or two-hour workout and exert himself to his fullest extent. He won't find himself in the middle of a workout saying, "Man, I've got to puke my guts out—I'm not in shape yet."

Your body has to be ready to specialize—you're handicapping yourself if you're not ready to do that. Gibby Hatton (Junior World Sprint Champion) came up and trained with us last year. That boy has a tremendous amount of ability, is a heck of a nice guy, and has all the qualities of a thoroughbred sprinter. I think he'll make an all-around bike rider, too—but he lacked physical fitness when he was up here. I hadn't been sprinting for a couple of years and he was a hair faster than me, but he couldn't stay in a pace line with us or go through all the jumps and sprints without feeling wiped out at the end. If it had come to a race, I could have beaten Gibby, even though he was faster than I was—simply because I was more physically fit.

When you come into a race, your pulse goes up and you're short of breath because your nerves are playing tricks on you, and if you're not physically fit you're going to handicap yourself and your reactions are going to be slower. Even in pursuiting, when the panic comes and the adrenaline starts rolling you can't control it if you're not physically fit. Even in training you can't control it. If you're doing a 4000-meter time trial for training and you're not physically fit, you won't have it under good control—you'll get to where the pain comes and start thinking, "Oh-oh, the pain's going to come, hope I don't throw up. I want to make a good time." You overemphasize and make dramatic impressions in your mind. Let's face it, athletes are a very dramatic type of people, very eccentric. Unless you're physically fit you're going to be cutting yourself short.

I think that no matter what the event is, track or road, before you specialize there should be a certain amount of fitness achieved. It takes about three months to get to that level, assuming you had good fitness the previous season. Before you can even get on the track there should first be a certain amount of road riding and road racing. Then you can get into the specialization and get the feel of it and start doing better times—it will come so much easier and be so much more fun and pleasurable. You'll accept high stress competition because you'll be physically and mentally capable of doing it—you'll have already put yourself through that sort of thing.

GB: Is it a fair conclusion that someone who wants to become a sprinter had just better find someone like Jack Disney and start asking questions?

Mountford: Yes—either that or go to Europe, but that's a big hassle: you've got to have money, contacts with people, a place to live and so on. There's a different environment, different languages, different food, everything, it's a whole different world.

I think the new rider has to have set in his mind a basic scheme that's been proved through time or sanctioned by people who've been through it already, like myself or like Jack Disney.

GB: If you had 10 prospective sprinters, you wouldn't give them all the same training program, would you?

Mountford: In the beginning, I would. I trained with Trentin and Morelon (French world champions) the one year I lived in Paris, under their coach "Toto" Gerardin and we all did the same thing. There's no secret about it–in fact, I used to train harder when I was with Jack Disney than when I was in France. In Paris we'd be there every day on the track at nine o'clock and start getting into our pace line. Sometimes there would be 50, sometimes 30—it was quite a large track—and the pace line would go for 50 laps. Every lap when a man would go off the front you'd count down: "He was 48, so the next guy will be 47," and so on, until it got down to about 10 and the pace was really going. A couple of sprinters would be dropping out and the pursuiters would be trying to burn off the sprinters, and at the end you sprinted toward the finish.

Then we'd pair off in twos or threes and do some jumps, maybe—just line up side by side and about 50 meters out Gerardin would blow the whistle and we'd jump for the finish line. Then we'd do a couple of sprints, and that was it. That would be happening every day at nine o'clock in the morning.

Every afternoon you were expected to be out on your own for about 30 miles on a good road ride. That was basically it, and if he saw that you were weak in one area or another he would tell you. Many times I'd come back in the afternoon because my jump wasn't strong enough, and go through about 10 strenuous jumps on the track. There's no special secret. It was all based on leadership and telling a guy he could do it—seeing that the other guy could do it, so you could do it too.

GB: Did Gerardin wait until later in the season to concentrate on correcting people's weaknesses?

Mountford: He'd do that all along. In the beginning of the season we would do mostly pacing and no sprinting for the first couple or three weeks—just pacing and finishing up with a sprint, and maybe jumps—basically physical fitness work. Sometimes he'd be sitting about three quarters of the way up the track on the turn, where he could see you as you were laid over really getting it on, and he would watch your position. He could see from there whether a rider was overstraining or not, whether he was too high or too low. For instance, he would study me and then afterwards come up and say, "Try and put your seat down half a centimeter." Then he'd tell me to lower it another half-centimeter and say, "Now you're looking good, now you're getting your heel and calf into the stroke more than you have been."

GB: Generally, do you believe that physical abilities like leg strength, spin and so on, which are reputed to be specific skills for track racing, come second to physical fitness?

Mountford: No, those things come at the beginning of the year. You can not get suppleness except through miles, miles and more miles. Eventually you develop suppleness so that you can pedal that 6½" crank around without fighting it. Suppleness comes when you pick up your leg and your calves feel like a ripe papaya or something. That means that you're in shape—your muscles are strong and yet they're supple enough that the blood can travel through your legs and you can work for a longer time. But if you don't have that suppleness and your legs are always tight, or maybe one muscle's tight, it's going to cut off circulation and you'll become tired. So why go and try to do something specialized if you don't have this suppleness in your legs? The suppleness, the breathing, the cardiovascular fitness—everything is done in the first months of training.

INTERVALS WITH EASE

BY MATT CRISTE

Matt Criste is one of those annoying "anti-trainers" who drive other racers nuts. The 1973 Northern California kilometer champion, Twilight Series winner and successful criterium specialist believes training should be fun and should take up a minimum of time. His ideas will be of special interest to the older rider, perhaps married and with heavy responsibilities, who wants to train for short-distance criterium racing without dedicating his whole free time to riding.

Matt holds an engineering degree and runs a custom motorcycle business. The 25-year-old veteran of three racing seasons injured his leg in 1971, ending a successful motorcycle racing career, and took up bike racing to stay active.

The way I got into intervals was that I discovered they worked for me, with my type of riding and the sort of rider that I am. The reason they work for me is that I am mainly interested in criterium riding. I feel criteriums are the way most beginning riders get involved in cycling. They probably see one, they want to get involved and interval training has a high yield of results for that sort of racing.

Another reason I do intervals is that the benefits are more apparent within a shorter period of time. The cost is a little bit higher in terms of fatigue and your attitude, and that's what this article is largely about—learning to live with intervals.

The purpose of intervals is to advance an individual's physical abilities and riding technique through a program of intense but short training, by similating racing conditions without racing fatigue. If you want to be a road rider, you've got to spend a lot of time in the saddle, whereas if you want to be a criterium rider you can ride long miles and be good, or you can have an interval program worked out and do just as well. Criterium riding closely approximates a certain type of interval schedule that I've worked out.

If you don't let yourself get fat and out of shape over the winter, I think you can start most of your riding in January. I'm sure I don't go more than 100 miles a week during the off-season and if you're a criterium specialist I don't think you need a lot of miles before you begin your real initial training in January.

I classify intervals into two types. One type I call "pure pain," and the other I call "simple pain." "Pure pain" is more like the classical interval that has come from Europe. It's almost always done on a circuit or a track—it's very intense, and you don't want to go meandering around. "Simple pain" you do on a larger circuit. I look at "simple pain" intervals as fun time. It's the kind of interval that's not quite as intense, and that you can go out and do with your buddies. Many riders just aren't capable of doing heavy intervals—it just destroys them and many don't have the attitude for it—and "simple pain" intervals are something they can live with.

I don't ever do "pure pain" intervals early in the year. The only time I do these is for a specific event. Let's say there's a race coming up, or I'm training for the kilometer or the Nationals or something. Then I'll go out with a friend—usually not with very many people either, as they may not be as serious as you are and that distracts your concentration. I always do "pure pain" on a circuit, as I mentioned before, and I always use a selected gear—usually it's a little bit bigger than I'd use for "simple pain." I keep a really close watch on my bodily functions—I watch my heartbeat and respiratory rate during those days I'm doing the intervals and of course I enter this information in my log book when I wake up in the morning; that way I can really see the results, and alter my program. If my resting heart rate rises in the morning I know it's time to ease off and rest.

People usually start riding on January 1—the magical day when they start logging their miles. I don't do that. And I don't go out and ride 100 miles a day on my road bike; I think that's a big waste of time, especially if your main interest isn't in road racing. I go to the bike shop every year and buy an old junky frame, an old Peugeot UO8 or something—my first one was a Flandria, a real tank. I like to fool around with bikes a lot, so I build a bike and I call it a "Masinelliago." I had a buddy and we thought we were so great that not one famous builder could build us a suitable bike—they'd all have to get together, the result being Masi, Cinelli and Colnago putting together this conglomerate.. So I go out and buy all the cheapest parts I can find and put the bike together for about $10 and put a fixed gear on it.

You start your "simple pain" training with a gear of around 63". That's the key. Some people go as low as 58", but you should never be higher than

John Howard leading a sprint—Matt Criste says it's times like this
when race-pace training pays off. (John Gordon)

65". This type of interval is rarely done on a short circuit; what you *don't*
want to do is go down and ride around on the track—that's really boring. I live
kind of far away from the track and when I go down there I don't want to spend
my time doing intervals—I can do those anywhere. I get my fixed gear set up, and
then I get three or four friends together—usually any more than that's no fun—
and make sure they can ride all the time as a group. If you go out one day and
there are only two of you or you go out and there are new faces, it doesn't seem
to work as well. The group isn't homogenous.

   With this type of riding it's not important to be very careful and monitor
your bodily functions, because that takes a lot of the fun out of it. Intervals
aren't really fun, so you've got to be careful about that. We ride north down El
Camino (a major north-south artery) into the wind, and then we cut over to a
frontage road and come back. The ride is only about 25 miles long, and we go
north because we're riding into the wind when we're fresh, then when we come
back the wind's on our tail and this tends to make us overspin when we otherwise wouldn't. I think this last part is really important, another key that I've
found to getting a good workout in a short time.

   What we do is try to get five or six sprints during this ride. We sprint for
city limit signs. There's a stretch up there where there's a city limit about every
two miles. What we do is, we get out and warm up for a few miles, then pick up
the pace 'til we're riding along trying to race with traffic, practicing our pace line.
We all know where the city limits are, so it's not a "jump" type of sprint, but

rather we wind it up and then we go real hard—I think it's a must that you get out of the saddle—and sprint for the city limits. You're all blown out after that —it's pretty tough in a 65" gear—then you all rest, get together, talk about it a little bit, what happened and who won this time and that sort of thing, then after you rest a little you get it together and go for the next city limits. I've found that if I do this four times a week, it's all the training I need. It's incredible. I can get on my road bike after having ridden a low fixed gear, and I can spin an 88"—unbelievable. During the off-season I play football and I train with weights, and that's the only other exercise I do to give me a base.

Real interval training is what I'd associate with "pure pain," where we go out and take our heartbeat then ride for a kilometer and come back. Say the kilometer takes us a minute and 12 seconds, so we rest for a minute and 12 seconds then go do another one. We do five of those, then rest for 20 minutes and recover completely—that's what I'd consider real intervals. "Simple pain" is actually a kind of interval, but it's tolerable for the novice rider or for a regular rider early in the year. The net result is similar to what a "pure pain" interval would give, only without the mental fatigue and the mental stress and the physical demands that would be put on you.

In the "simple pain" type of course it's good to have a hill or two, and sprint for the bottom of the hill. I feel it's really good to over-rev—I don't think a lot of riders ever turn their gears over 100 rpm. That's why they train hard and do ok in a race, but when it comes to the sprint it's guys like me who have half their miles in who're able to win—simply because I know what it is to rev really high—I can identify with the feeling.

You may wonder how I go about getting a frame for a Masinelliago. Near the end of the season you just start looking around for them—they're everywhere, and they're really cheap. Anything'll work—it doesn't really matter. You're using such a low gear that you can haul just about anything around. I tried clinchers last year, and they worked ok.

In the Italian system of training they always employ a fixed gear—around the third month of training they allow you to start riding a freewheel. I've found that if I go out and ride my fixed gear the day before a race it really helps. I'll go out and do a couple of sprints in a low gear, and it really makes a difference. I don't think you need to make more than two gear changes during the season, and I don't think you should ever ride on anything higher than an 80" gear for the type of training that I'm suggesting.

I add "pure pain" intervals later in the season, for specific results in a race. I don't think you should start them any later than 4-5 days before the race, because you can't recover from them easily.

I have several circuits I use to help make intervals fun. One is the "Daily Sprint Circuit." That's the one where we go up El Camino and sprint for the city limit signs. Then we come back and draft the mail truck on the frontage road, which takes the speed up a little.

Another game we play is called "Catch Eddy Merckx." Maybe a mile or two before the city limit sign, if we're tired of just sprinting as usual, we'll spend one guy off and say he's Eddy Merckx. We get all psyched up about how we've got to catch him, and then we just jam as hard as we can. Usually a couple of guys will come off the back, and if we catch him we feel really good about it, squirting him with our water bottles and all that sort of thing—that's the key to it, if you keep it light you can tolerate the hard riding.

I like to motorpace, and we have a system that lets us incorporate our interval training with motorpacing. I was doing this with Tim Nicholson, a really good rider to work with. What I'd do is find a circuit like the Redwood City criterium course, and one rider would go out behind the motorcycle and go around for a few laps, picking his speed up until he was pretty tired, then he'd drop off and the other rider would sprint behind the motor, which is like intervals with work and then a rest; and you also get the advantage of a good draft with the motorpacing.

We've got another course in a swank residential area here where we go if the traffic is really heavy or we can't ride our regular course at the usual time. By the way, time is very important—I think you should do intervals only in the afternoon or evening, because otherwise you tend to be a little bit fagged-out for the rest of the day. This circuit is about a kilometer around and there's one place where you go downhill with an overspin. We call it "Tooth Alley," because one of my teeth fell out going down there. We have these nicknames that kind of make it fun and a little more tolerable.

I think you should only attempt intervals after you have some base mileage. You don't want to go out and start doing this sort of thing suddenly because you'll tear up all the muscles in your legs—it's good to learn first how to breathe properly and get your form together. And I don't think you should do intervals unless you have a goal established. There was one kid who wanted to race bicycles who'd come out with us, but he didn't really know what he was training for. He didn't like to go out there and have it hurt, and not know why he was hurting. By comparison, for example, I knew the glory of winning so I could go out there and say, "Wow, this really hurts, but I know it's going to pay off when I win the race and get all these tires and all this prestige, and it'll qualify me for the nationals." I think it's important for this intensive, hurting type of training, that you've got to have a goal. Otherwise, you can't do it very long.

Of course, a rider has to be in proper physical and mental health. If you've got problems at home or you've got a cold, you'd better stay home. And I think you should ride "simple pain" intervals with good friends, while for "pure pain" you should ride by yourself or with people you hate. I find that if I ride by myself it's very good because I really can get into it. I can take all the time I want and really get prepared. But if I ride with friends, we're apt to talk and kid around a little and that breaks your concentration. If you're riding with people that you don't like you want to beat them and you'll extend yourself a little bit —you'll try a little harder. Tim Nicholson was running an interval session down at East Meadow Circle, and he was one guy I always wanted to beat, so when he was there I'd be all hot to go down and race him. I'd notice that in the race the weekend after that I'd really feel good because I'd tried real hard.

During the actual racing season, in May or June, I find that I don't need to ride my bike in training more than a couple of times a week. On Thursday night I ride the Twilight Series training race, then Saturday I can go to the track, and Sunday's a race. So that leaves Monday, Tuesday, Wednesday and Friday. I would always ride the fixed gear a couple of those days, and maybe one of the buddies would call up and want to go for a ride in the hills to keep things interesting. I remember in '73 some times when I only rode in the races and that was all.

I do a lot of isotonic exercises and I jump rope at work. I used to do boxing and have been involved with a lot of sports. I've found that there's always some bit of information from the previous sport that I can use to my advantage in the new sport, to abbreviate the time that I have to spend in training. Fencing really helped me with cycle racing for instance, with the leg exercises you have to do, and with boxing the workouts I had to do with a jump rope were really good also. You can do intervals with the jump rope—to go three minutes as fast as you can is really tough. I do some of these things at work and they supplement my bicycle racing.

The "simple pain" type of interval is all that a novice rider should think about. He shouldn't even consider the "pure pain" type—it's too much. After a "simple pain" workout I feel really good. You should never totally exhaust yourself—that's really important for training rides. You should feel tired and kind of tingley all over.

Interval training goes hand in hand with weight training and massotherapy. You're doing damage to your muscle fibers and massotherapy is very important if you're looking for optimum results. The novice can't get involved with this sort of thing, though—there's too much knowledge involved and too much time to be spent with it, so I feel it's better if he doesn't get wrapped up in it.

To be a really top-level road racer demands an awful lot of time—as much as three or four hours a day on the bike. This is just about impossible for the family man or student, and I believe "simple pain" intervals may be the ultimate answer for opening the door to bike racing for those of us who just can't give it our all.

INGREDIENTS OF LSD

BY GEORGE BEINHORN

Readers unfamiliar with the various schools of training theory will be shocked to learn that many cyclists do "LSD workouts" to increase their endurance. No, they're not cycling high—they're just following a training method known as Long Slow Distance. The term "LSD" was coined by *Runner's World* magazine editor Joe Henderson in a book for distance runners titled *Long Slow Distance—The Humane Way to Train*, in which he advocated a turning away from hard and fast training methods which were popular at the time. At the opposite extreme from LSD is something that's been called "POT," for "Plenty of Tempo." Like most of our training ideas in cycling, the "fast and hard" idea has come to us from sports physiologists working with runners. The most common version of POT is interval training, developed by Dr. Reindell in Germany and associated through the years with coaches Mihaly Igloi, Waldemar Gerschler, Franz Stampfl and the Freiburg training group. LSD's leading advocates have been internationally famous distance running coaches Arthur Lydiard of New Zealand, Bill Bowerman of the University of Oregon and Dr. Ernst van Aaken of Waldniel, Germany.

The battle between LSD and POT has been long and vicious. Nowhere has it raged more fiercely than in Germany, where a good deal of professorly dignity and pride have prevented constructive communication between the sophisticated thinkers representing each side. Accordingly, modifications in the extremes have come not from research labs and theoretical papers, but from results obtained out on the roads, tracks and playing fields. Pure interval training produced literally thousands of cases of stress fatigue and early retirement from sport, disappointing race results and serious health problems such as a condition called energic-dynamic cardiac insufficiency in which one part of the heart is developed more than others, with a consequent dangerous imbalance.

Pure LSD advocates have encountered stagnation and lack of improvement. Where interval advocates are now recommending a healthy base of endurance work and much more gentle programs of speed work, the LSD people are saying that an athlete must realize that his long slow distance pace gradually increases, and that he'll only improve by exercising at his "optimally slow" pace—just at the outside edge of endurance levels.

Speed work is described elsewhere in this book, but since even Matt Criste's pure interval method depends on a thorough base of endurance, and since the research indicates that resistance to fatigue over long distances can't be attained safely by short and fast work alone, we're going to look at the theoretical basis of LSD training, and the important work that's done by your body while it rests.

IMPROVING YOUR ENERGY EFFICIENCY

Energy for all physical activity is produced in two different ways: with oxygen or without oxygen. The oxygen-supplied way is commonly called "aerobic" energy production, or "biological oxidation." Oxygenless energy production is called "anaerobic" or "glycolysis."

Warburg found in the '30s that when oxygen is in short supply all mammalian tissue breaks down sugar for energy. This is "glycolysis," and it begins anytime respiration is cut off or the organism is working so hard that oxygen is in short supply.

A fresh supply of oxygen has the opposite effect: it stops the process of glycolysis. This is called the "Pasteur Effect." Glycolysis—exercise without oxygen—can never permanently replace biological oxidation, certainly not in endurance sports. You eventually have to stop and catch your breath when you go at sprint pace.

ATP is a major energy-holding compound in the body. When one compares the amount of ATP produced during biological oxidation and during glycolysis. it turns out that 19 times as much sugar must be burned up by glycolysis to produce the same amount of energy that could be supplied by the process of biological oxidation.

What this means is that exercise done at a degree of effort that makes you short of breath uses up about 19 times as much stored energy per unit of work as exercise done at aerobic, easy-breathing pace. Glycolysis produces 36 kcal of energy from one mole of glucose, while the same amount of glucose produces 672 kcal by biological oxidation.

Glycolysis is an emergency function of the cell. The result of heavy interval training on the bicycle, for instance, is loss of stored glycogen and also a pathological condition called creatinuria, plus the stressful mental and physical effects of frequent excesses of lactic acid in the blood. These factors—destruction of energy stores and lactic acid formation—account respectively for the "burned-out" periods often encountered by athletes who do a lot of intense intervals, and the mental depression that can also attend too frequent speed workouts. Note that Matt Criste's recommended training is done only four days a week at most, allowing abundant time for the body to recover from the hard work involved.

Dr. van Aaken of the Waldniel LSD group points out a further danger of speed: "In interval damaged runners, who all showed considerable creatinuria as well as increased expulsion of potassium and phosphates, an energic-dynamic heart insufficiency could be considered probable—particularly in light of the fact that with continuously increasing heart volume, proportional drops in performance were registered." Intervals increase the heart's stroke volume, but at the expense of the heart's overall efficiency and health.

"With harmonious growth of the heart as in moderate endurance training," van Aaken continues, "surface growth is relatively favorable and coronary circulation remains proportional. Hypoxia (lack of oxygen) in the heart muscle, which must never appear in endurance training but is actually provoked in interval training, accelerates the release of potassium and, conversely, the absorption of sodium and water. Increased losses of potassium from the heart muscle can cause fiber edema and interstitial edema, which in turn may lead to a weakening of the heart."

Athletes who've overdone their speed work have provided van Aaken for years with ammunition for his battle with his Freiburg rivals. The history of running during the '50s and '60s is littered with dozens of big names who've overdone their speed, suffering stress fractures, regressing performances, months-long layoffs, failing enthusiasm and inexplicable ups and downs in race performance. World record miler Jim Ryun, well known for his heavy interval sessions, has never recovered the form he had when he ran his amazing 3:51.1. During recent seasons he's run 3:58 one day and an "inexplicable" 4:12 the next.

Even the Freiburg group, first and last bastion of interval training, have watered their official program to the point where it strongly resembles the endurance method. Like van Aaken and Lydiard, they now recommend a very large foundation of aerobic work with application of intervals only for seasonal "sharpening" before big races.

WHAT'S THE ANSWER?

We've looked at the dangers of speed. What's the training that replaces repeat sprints?

Van Aaken's explanations of LSD are particularly interesting because they take matters right down to the cell level: "Myoglobin, the major storer of oxygen, presents itself as the basis of modern endurance performance. Increasing our myoglobin and hemoglobin supplies is a key factor in developing energy production capacity.

"Endurance training creates an increase in aerobic metabolism including my-oglobin stores, by keeping stresses constantly at the point of optimal breathing efficiency." By "optimal breathing efficiency" van Aaken is referring to the "conversational pace" commonly known among endurance-trained athletes. The idea is to ride as hard as you can without getting so out of breath that you can't still comfortably hold a conversation. This speed increases slowly, perhaps only a few miles per hour per year, but small gains in this kind of basic aerobic efficiency represent a significantly improved ability to store energy. Your training speed rises slowly, but your ability to go long distances at race pace increases most quickly by this method.

Two reservations to the panacea of long slow distance are specific to cycling. The first is time. Van Aaken says a cyclist who wants to compete at top international level will have to ride 5-5½ hours per day. Not only is this far too boring for most of us, but who's got the time? Several alternatives are possible: early season running to establish an endurance base, which is then maintained by work on the bike; settling for less; criterium specialization as described by Matt Criste.

The other reservation is the specific need in cycling to work on spin, jump ability, a finishing sprint. There's no other way to do this than by active practice, which unavoidably resembles interval training. Criste claims he can win races from riders with many more miles in their legs than he has, because of his strong sprint finish and ability to spin hard and fast. The Stetina brothers spend hundreds of miles working on their spin in low gears. Obviously, the Stetinas have been cycling very well without getting burned out. The reason may lie in some facts about anaerobic, fast-paced cycling that haven't been yet investigated by sports medicine. Swimmers have known for years that they can do interval repetitions that make runners who hear about them gape in open-mouthed astonishment. The difference seems to lie in the buoyant "assist" a swimmer gets from the water in which he exercises, and perhaps also in the combinations of muscle groups he uses. Intervals which raise the heart rate to the same levels as those encountered by runners seem to be tolerated better by swimmers. And the same thing appears to happen in cycling. We can't overlook the possible heart damage of which van Aaken warns, but it may be justified to say on the basis of top racers' experience that a moderate interval program gives less risk of a burnout for cyclists than for runners.

Endurance training aims at maximum use of oxygen from the smallest volume of air—a sure sign of enhanced myoglobin availability. Myoglobin supplies are most efficiently developed at an exercising heart rate of between 120-140, which varies between individuals. Coaches who teach endurance training also advise the athlete to lose weight, creating more favorable endurance and heart quotients. Marathon runners have encountered a 5% increase in aerobic (easy-breathing) running speed for every 5% drop in body weight. Weight loss will have obvious advantages for the cyclist, and it's notable that most of the recent crop of "Super Juniors" are lightweights—with a powerful motor in a trimmed-down body.

"The heart's volume is increased in endurance training through continuous low-intensity stresses over a period of, for example, two to six years," says van Aaken. There doesn't seem to be any getting around it—there's no substitute for miles.

YOU TRAIN EVEN WHILE YOU SLEEP

A number of physiologists and doctors of sports medicine have made the subject of rest their specialty. Dr. van Aaken dwells at length on the importance of adequate recovery from exercise, reknowned physiologist Hans Selye, author of the classic *Stress of Life*, has made it his life's work, and now the Russians have become interested. Drs. N. V. Grayevskaya and L. A. Joffe of the Scientific Research Institute of Physical Culture in Moscow authored a paper on the subject which appeared in an official Russian sports technical journal.

The Russian investigators say that two things can happen when you rest between training sessions: 1. Your body can adapt to the work done, getting ready for more work by storing energy-binding compounds and improving all its performance-related systems; or 2. The work can be too much for the body's stress adaptation mechanisms to handle. Because of insufficient time between workouts, lack of sleep, not enough relaxation, emotional stresses, poor diet and so on, the body may not be able to "meet the challenge" between training rides. When the second process happens, you begin to develop symptoms of overstress: runny nose, sore muscles, irritability, lack of enthusiasm, restless sleep, diarrhea, etc.

To make sure your recovery is complete you have to take into account all the factors involved in recovery. This is where the Russian scientists' paper on "Theoretical and Practical Aspects of The Problem of Recovery" can help us out.

FACTORS OF EDUCATION

This concerns the way you put together your training program. You have to realize very clearly, for example, that it's dangerous folly to be too ambitious. Eddy Merckx's training works for him, but would probably be beyond the capacities of any living American cyclist. Merckx's stress adaptation ability astonishes his doctors; the Belgian King of the Roads is an amazingly fast healer.

An article in Britain's *Cycling* magazine by Belgian correspondent Marcel De Leneer quoted Eddy Merckx's trainer Lucien Acou who advised young cyclists to stay well within their own safe capacities in training: "It is vital that you don't overtrain or race too often before the body has stopped growing." Acou dissuaded Merckx from riding amateur stage races like the Tour de l'Avenir and Peace Race, and he claims this has allowed Eddy's stamina to develop uninterruptedly through the years so that he now outclasses other riders who "feel the effects of doing too much when they were younger." "Stage races," says Acou, "force youngsters to dig deep into their natural reserves. They cannot have enough time to recover."

"Factors of education" include training theory, stress awareness, and common sense experience. Over the years you'll learn how far you can push yourself under an endless variety of conditions you'll face in training and racing: little sleep, hot weather, freezing cold rain, extra-long training miles when you don't feel like it but which you've scheduled (should you or shouldn't you?). Older athletes tend to be uncoached—they're educated to coach themselves for the most part, by listening to their body's inner wisdom.

There are no generalized rules for training. You can spin a 74" gear while someone else can spin 83". Are you going to listen to their advice to train on a higher cog? Not if it strains you to the point where your recovery is incomplete.

Training takes thought, experience, intelligent use of the brain—it's not an intuitive thing at first, but requires education.

MEDICAL AND BIOLOGICAL FACTORS

These include diet, race drinks, massage and so on. Optimizing each one, taking the right kind and amount of each rather than "as much as possible," increases the body's ability to recover quickly from the stresses of training and competition.

Grayevskaya and Joffe list other areas where biological factors can be important: "removal of general and specific fatigue, rapid replenishment of energy reserves, intensification of tissue synthesis, optimization of the body's vitamin balance, restoration of defense adaptation mechanisms, increase of stability in the face of specific and non-specific training influences."

Medical and biological factors make the body a more efficient machine, according to the Russians. The body is able to recover more quickly between training sessions, allowing the athlete to do more without risking overstress. Wrong food or too much food, for instance, puts stress loads on the body, robbing energy from its adaptive mechanisms. The Stetinas claim a vegetarian raw foods diet has greatly improved their ability to recover from races and hard training.

PSYCHOHYGIENIC FACTORS

Hans Selye lists mental and psychological tensions among the stress factors that decrease our efficiency and sap our energy. The Russian paper recommends as ways of preventing psycho-nervous energy loss "psycho-regulatory and autogenic training, sleep therapy, special films, exercises for muscle relaxation and removal of negative psychological feators. Yoga seems to fit the bill. The yogic stretches release physical tensions which are caused by emotional and mental inharmonies, and tend by a kind of reversal or feedback to remove the original troubles, making the mind relaxed and harmonious. We're not aware of the "special films" referred to by the Russians.

"Negative psychological factors" are stresses like anger, jealousy, resentment, grief, depression which can be removed by a number of psychological methods. A study by the Stanford Research Institute found meditation to be one of the most potent anti-stress techniques. It's now being practiced by a number of top American riders, who've found it gives the heart, lungs and brain a deep, satisfying rest.

Grayevskaya and Joffe's paper points to the importance of avoiding unnecessary stresses, which give the body "too much to digest" between workouts." "Important information about the influence of recovery on the athlete's condition can be obtained by reading his training diary and observing the way he feels, the amount of sleep he's getting, his weight, appetite, desire for training and eagerness to compete." The old axiom that "whatever hurts must be doing me some good" has been proved false—the cult of pain has been replaced by the cult of balance.

MOTORPACING : EXTRA EDGE

BY WALLY SUMMERS

After a 13-year stint in the British amateur ranks during which time he rode every distance from quarter-mile to 24-hour events, winning some track championships and proving himself one of the best hill climbers, "Wally" Summers turned professional in 1945, but not before becoming one of the original rebels who started road racing proper on British roads during World War II.

Mr. Summers has ridden in three World Championships as a pace-follower, or as it is known in Europe "stayer." He was a finalist in Paris in 1947 and was considered one of the eight best European stayers for several years.

Wally Summers is no stranger to road racing either. He rode in the Tour de Suisse three times, all alone without a team. He finished 38th in 1948—about two hours on overall classification behind the famous Ferdi Kubler. Wally also set up the first British Pembroke-to-London road record of 11 hours, 48 minutes for the 248 miles. He then broke every motor-paced track record on the books from one to 50 miles and considers one of his best rides the British 50-mile paced record which still stands to him in one hour, 13 minuts.

Summers has raced in 23 different countries. The Union Cycliste Internationale turned him down for what he had hoped would be his last World Championship ride, mainly because of his age (60) and the fact that he has the heart murmur typical of so many athletes. Wally was chagrined to say the least as in July of 1974 just before setting out for Montreal and the World Champions he covered a 50-kilometer course in 51 minutes on the road near his Tucson, Ariz., home. And in September of 1973 he rode from Phoenix to Tucson motor-paced in seven hours. The distance is 125 miles and climbs gradually over 2,000 feet. The weather was over 100 degrees at the time. In Montreal on the super-fast steeply banked board track Wally was registering lap times in training right up to the day before the race equal to those of the winner of the championship, Cees Stam of Holland.

Does pacing a motorcycle help a roadman in training? Well, one has only to refer to Monsieur Eddy Merckx for the answer. Eddy flew over to Mexico City in October of 1972 after a most hectic road racing season, with the aim of capturing a new world record for the hour unpaced ride. Upon arrival at the Olympic Stadium in Mexico quite adverse weather conditions set in, making track work impossible and normal road training dubious, With only a few days at his disposal to acclimatize to the "thin air," the problem seemed acute.

In short order a motorcycle was conjured up, complete with safety roller at the rear, and Merckx proceeded to train behind it on a closed circuit riding the intermittent periods without rain. He was doing what comes naturally to most European riders, professional and amateur: pace-following for training in lieu of

Summers working out behind his pacer. The rider should be so close to the roller that to a bystander it looks as if he's actually touching it—but this kind of precision takes time to develop.

riding with a fast bunch of training partners. Long in vogue with both road and track riders, motorcycle-assisted training is accepted in all the great cycling countries as a most useful asset. Incidentally, Merckx actually put in several fast laps on the track behind his motorcycle as a warmup before riding to capture a new world unpaced hour record.

At the 1974 World Cycling Championships in Montreal, it was interesting to note that sometimes as many as 15 riders of all nationalities could be seen strung out behind a single medium-size motorcycle. Of course it is obvious that behind a pacemaker-motorcycle consistent lap times can be established on the track, not only for one rider but for several.

But what about roadmen in the ordinary sense? Can they benefit without recourse of traveling to a track? Yes, they can. A good road racing cyclist, especially one who lives isolated from any regular opportunity to train with a fast bunch, will benefit greatly from a regular weekly schedule of paced training. His main problem will be to find a willing motorcyclist friend keen enough to devote the time and adapt himself to some simple requirements.

As the motorcycle is the essential tool, let's deal with it first. It should not be a mini-bike, as some of these "wee beasties" can easily be outrun by a good racing cyclist. A medium to large machine is desirable, hopefully without "moto-cross" upswept exhaust and excessive noise problems.

The main item and most important alteration of the motorcycle is a steel safety roller usually not less than about 2½ inches in diameter and about two feet long, so that it is about as wide as the outermost part of the motorcycle. This roller should be on good bearings and spin with the minimum of touch. It should be fixed to the motorcycle in the strongest fashion possible and the height of the roller should be at a level with the front hub of the racing cycle's front wheel. *Never* ride behind a motorcycle without a safety roller. For a racing man to touch the rear wheel of a rapidly moving motorcycle can be disastrous.

Before embarking on your first training ride a "bull session" is essential between your pacemaker and yourself. A mode of communication has to be agreed upon as lots of shouting back and forth can be both confusing and dangerous to the concentration required to follow your pace safely and consistently. Shouting takes a lot of much-needed breath from the racing cyclist. The international dialogue, used almost without exception, is simple. For increased speed a rider shouts "Allez!" and to slacken off speed he shouts "Ho!" For example, in the need for a rapid sprint, "Allez-Allez!" at which time the pacemaker in the motorcycle turns his throttle for increased speed, but in a gradual fashion so that his following rider is not left chasing a fast-departing motorcycle along the road or track.

Assuming that you have the roller adequately fixed up on your friend's motorcycle and that you both fully understand your decided-upon means of communication (you may as well use the simple international code as it has been found that a rider can aspirate both Allez and Ho with a minimum of breath), the next step is to essay out onto the road. For heaven's sake choose a quiet stretch of highway, preferably without many side streets that let traffic filter on, and of course a road that does not have continual traffic light controls and stop signs. A stretch of 20 miles of secluded highway is fine, 30 miles is even better.

Now you are eager to start, but first make sure your tires are securely stuck to the rims of your racing bicycle. The best professionals and amateurs use a shellac coating, as many as 12 coats on the rim and three or four on the base of the tire. The wheel rim should be roughed up with a round file before any adhesive is applied; this gives the adhesive something to grip on. If you must use the rim cement so popular with roadmen, then make sure you give both tire and rim several applications depending on the texture of the cement in question. A tire used for pace-following, front or rear, should be on the rim so firmly that it takes quite a bit of manual labor to remove it. A blowout or tire leaving the rim at speed through lack of adhesion has provided many a trackman and roadman with a decidedly painful lesson.

On the subject of tires for paced training, avoid those ultra-light ones and use preferably a tire of about 260 grams weight. Naturally, make sure the remainder of the road racing bicycle is in tip-top shape. Handlebars and saddle must be secure, wheels firmly locked in the frame, and brake levers where you can get at them without too much contortion. Light fingering of the brakes will be necessary while you are getting accustomed to following closely behind the roller on the motorcycle.

A normal 10-speed racing bike is OK for paced training, but avoid too much gear changing. You should not train on a hilly course if it can be avoided, as the essence of paced training is to develop tempo for your normal road and track racing. Use your somewhat higher top gears as you will find the "drafting" effect of pacing allows for a higher speed than unpaced work. Try and stick to one of the high gears; a good gear is 56 x 15 (100.8") if you have this combination, otherwise it is your decision and what best suits you. Avoid low gears, though. The smaller gears produce too much jockeying on the saddle and consequently crotch chafing that can be bothersome.

Above all else *do not* alter the basic frame of the bicycle. Turning forks back to front is very dangerous and putting a small wheel in the front forks does not enhance the steering of a road bike. The special bikes you see for pace following on the track are made that way, but they are much heavier, rigid and the front forks are specially curved to the rear and highly reinforced as are the wheels, saddle, handlebars, etc.

What about distance and speed, now that you are ready to train behind the motor? To start with, aim for a very slow first training ride. Get used to fanning the roller without "clobbering" it with your front wheel. To keep hitting the roller puts a decided brake on your legs and of course will wear the front tire down eventually. You will find that about 25 mph is a reasonable speed to start training with. It will seem slow sometimes, but the art of following has to be learned and it doesn't come overnight. You have to learn to ease slightly on your pedalling rhythm to maintain a close distance from the roller, and you have to learn to feather your brakes gently and not "grab" at them needlessly.

The whole art is to ride so close to the roller that it appears to the bystander that you are actually "rubbing" it all the time. Learn to seek your pacemaker's body shelter by drifting to one side or the other of the roller, making sure you do not drift over the end of it. Never override the motorcycle at the side. *Do not* start watching your revolving pedals—it could be fatal. And above all else, never train behind the motor without a crash helmet.

Wear track gloves, good shoes, shorts with a chamois insert seat and leg warmers if it is cold. Usually the "pros" wear a couple of jerseys even in the warm weather. This soaks up sweat and saves chafing under the arms and across the chest. It is surprising how "chafing" is the scourge of pace-following riders and also in how many peculiar places chafing can arise, especially over long distance events.

3

Riding
The Track

BY BARRY HARVEY

British-born Barry Harvey started racing in 1960 at age 20—a late start by some standards, but graced with phenomenal early successes. While Harvey acknowledges his 20 wins in major events during his first year might have been the result of some native ability, he attributes his years at or near the top and his eight Canadian track championship "golds" to rigorous and scientific mental and physical preparation. Barry's racing career was interrupted by a serious injury while training for the 1972 Olympics.

Harvey was one of the first to promote the use of titanium in cycling, and he is now an executive in the "white collar" end of the sport as Bicycle Sales Manager for Teledyne. However, he still rides, perhaps harder than his doctors think he should, serves as media commentator and announcer for major US races and fits in as much track coaching as a busy schedule allows.

The modern track bike is the thoroughbred descendant of the basic "safety" bike of the 1880s. It has no brakes and a fixed single gear. For pursuit specialists there are super-light frames, but the standard sprint track frame is usually built heavier than comparable road models. It is the lack of brakes, freewheel blocks and derailleur sets that make track bikes lighter than the road machines. The bike will have more upright angles, less fork rake, a shorter wheel base and a higher bottom bracket than most road bikes. Though square road handlebars are now often used on the tracks, many riders still prefer the sprint pattern bars, which are more curved and deeper.

It is not my intention to go into detail regarding equipment. Perhaps young racers now think too much about getting the latest and lightest in equipment and not enough about perfecting their bodies and minds to make the best use of it. Though you should not expect costly bikes and gear to win races for you, every effort should be made to get first rate equipment, learn its best use and proper maintenance, and keep it in first class condition.

A few racing sessions will demonstrate that with the exception of an occasional puncture, not many top class riders lose races due to mechanical troubles. Their whole approach to the sport is disciplined. That is why they are champions

—not just by luck for one race or event, but by design, race after race, and sometimes year after year. Riders who take chances with faulty equipment deserve to lose, and usually do lose.

Track racing and training can take place on any well finished piece of straightway that can be kept free of auto traffic—a road, a street or an airfield runway. However, the races are meant for, and compeititon generally takes place on a special type of closed track: a "velodrome," in French "the home of the velos (bicycles)." There are three basic types of track:

Unbanked. Usually a running track with a cinder or composition surface, and usually a quarter mile or so in circumference. These are "slow," and put a high premium on maneuvers and psychological warfare. England has a number of grass surfaced tracks of this type, and they have their own national championships over ½-mile and five miles.

Shallow Banked. Most American tracks are of this type, being built either years ago when this was a world-wide style or built more recently to meet the ideas of park commissioners and the like who require a safe place for the kiddies to ride their Stingrays while the trackies are away. These are generally surfaced with concrete or asphalt, and range from three laps to the mile to 1/6-mile in circumference with banking from less than 15° to more than 30°.

Steeply Banked. These are usually 10 or 12 laps to the mile indoor "teacups" for professional racing, often designed to be portable and moved from venue to venue. The current UCI-approved Olympic and recommended World Championship 333.3-meter tracks are to be of this type, with turns banked to 55° and at least 40° required to keep the bikes on the track. Tracks of this quality, even for outdoor use, are usually built of wood, surfaced with rare and expensive hardwood boards. The development of US track racing has reached the point where the lack of a world-class track in the States is beginning to be keenly felt.

The tracks themselves are marked in a standardized manner. A start-finish line goes across the entire track width, with some tracks having more than one finish line marked to suit various distance events such as the kilometer and 4,000-meter pursuit.

A "pole line" is painted around the entire track a few inches above the inner boundary. This represents the shortest official legal distance around the track, and riders must ride on or above this line.

Next, 32 inches up the track slope, is the "safety line" running parallel to the pole line. A racer on or below this line is not to be passed on the inside, and a racer inside this line is not supposed to swing out of it during the last 200 meters of a race. Track tactics depend in good part on the use of these rules. It is common practice to refer to the entire track area between the pole and safety lines as the "pole" or "pole position."

The "relief line" runs parallel to the others about halfway up the banking. In team events the relief or non-competing racer should stay above this mark, and during training sessions slower moving riders should also keep above this line as a safety precaution.

THE EVENTS

Many track events can draw a crowd and are worthy of intense competition.

They range from six-day Madison style team racing, through handicapped races and variations on the pursuit and man-against-clock events. However, those that are recognized as events for World Championships by the Union Cycliste Internationale (UCI) are few in number, and those given National Championship status by the Amateur Bicycle League of America (ABL of A) are fewer still.

The Sprint. A match race over 1000 meters for two or more riders, decided by the best of three races after several rounds of elimination heats. One of the hardest things for spectators and beginners to learn is that in a sprint race it only matters if you are first at the finish, nowhere else, and from the nature of the human machine and the factors involved in such a race being first "most of the time" —leading for most of the race—rarely means crossing the finish line first. Tactics and bike handling are as important in sprinting as are physical strength and sheer speed.

The Kilometer. A pure time trial event with only one racer on the track at a time riding against the clock and against the times of other racers. The "kilo" is ridden from a standing start, without being pushed off or thrown by the rider's handler. The usual technique is to sprint away from the start, and it takes a specialist's skill not to "die" in the closing half lap or so. One thousand meters can seem a very long distance to a racer without stamina or training in the event.

The Pursuit. Professionals ride 5000 meters, Senior Men 4000 meters, and Women and Juniors 3000 meters. This is an individual event, and also one for a team of four. The racers or teams start on opposite sides of the track from a standing start and finish at the same points. The race is won by the first finisher (or in the case of a team pursuit, the third finisher on the winning team) crossing his line first, or by catching the other racer or team for a sudden death immediate victory. In the case of well-matched racers or teams the "pursuit" usually doesn't work, and the race goes its full distance, often being decided by time differences of only hundredths of a second.

Mass Start. Most English-speaking countries include a mass start track event in their championships, traditional in their cycling history since the turn of the century, but long since cut by the continentals and UCI. The usual distance is 10 miles, and race tactics are a mixture of sprinters' moves and road race maneuvers.

PERSONAL PREPARATION

For training as well as competition it is essential to have clothing that fits well. The clothing should be the best that can be afforded. The lift in morale for the "well turned out" racer, and clothing's effect on the opposition are not to be slighted. However, the fit is of most importance. Irritation and chaffing that can spoil a session or even a season may result from a poorly fit pair of shoes.

It is important that jerseys or track suit tops have adequate length to keep the small of the back covered. If there is a gap between the shorts and jersey perspiration will collect there allowing the small of the back to become chilled, with possible serious after-effects. Experienced trackies often wear a "T" or undershirt or even a second jersey under their racing jersey. This isn't just for warmth; in the event of a crash the outer jersey invariably slides on the under one, and while their jersey is ripped to shreds the racer will normally avoid major body abrasions.

Track mitts should always be worn, racing or training. There is nothing more uncomfortable than the deep scrapes to the palms that might result from even minor falls without protection for the hands.

Your life may depend on your helmet. Don't use the minimum flimsy leather hat that will just pass ABL and local regulations. While there are many improved models of the various plastic "soupbowl" types on the market now that will do a first rate job of protection, if you find you prefer a regular padded leather crash hat invest in one with adequate padding and coverage, making sure the straps fit behind and in front of the ears.

STYLE

The prime goal is a position on your bike that affords maximum efficiency. You must work around the following criteria:

● First consideration must go to balance. The rider's weight should be evenly distributed. The arms should not support the weight of the body, nor should they be overextended in reaching for the handlebars. Leg action should be fluid, and should neither go past normal flat-footed extension or show much hump at the knee at the bottom of the pedal stroke.

● Saddle height is best found by sitting the rider on his machine with his heels on his pedals at their lowest position. The leg should be straight, and I think the saddle should be dead level. On really small tracks and on rough ones it may help your control to have the saddle further back over the wheel than is road racing standard.

● Arm and body position is the most difficult to establish and might take a great deal of riding to find. Work toward a comfortable balance of weight between your arms and body. Ideally the weight distribution should be 45% on the front and 55% on the rear wheel.

It was my practice to take a few weeks after the season holiday from bikes and racing. I never had the funds for sufficient dissipation to go badly out of training, and short layoffs seemed to keep me from going mentally stale during the long track racing seasons. There are some who must keep grinding out the training miles throughout the year, though. This, like so much else in cycling will depend on your own bodily and mental makeup. None of these rules or training formulas are going to be 100% true in all cases for all riders. Everything sugested has to be considered in terms of you: *your* time, *your* effort, *your* plans and *your* body and mind.

Most of the training patterns I recommend are of the interval type. They worked well for me, and some of the best trackies I rode against use similar training regimens. This isn't the only way to train, and I don't offer it as the final word handed down from the gods or godlike experts.

As for the current popularity of LSD (Long Slow Distance) I and my training companions didn't train in that manner, so I have no practical appreciation of

Carl Leusenkamp is about to come around Barry Harvey during the semifinals of the sprint at the '71 Pan-American Team Trials. (Dick Vann Photo)

how it works. There may be some validity to cutting down the frequency of performing to optimum outputs in training; but, especially for sprinters and short distance road men, I cannot see eliminating the high stressed, flat out, training interval completely. LSD training certainly sounds a less demanding, more fun way to train, and if a racer could be sure everyone he's going to compete against follows the Long Slow Distance program, I would feel more comfortable about recomending it. However, I have seen too many races, road and track, won by a sprinter's jump and quick burst of high speed effort perfected by interval type training.

TRAINING THEORY

While it's important to keep racing a sport, and to take pleasure in what you are doing, I feel the most useful training programs still involve a considerable amount of simple suffering. Interval style training is probably the most economical of time and effort expended, but seems the hardest form of training there is. It takes many forms and can be adopted to suit your available time, physical make-up and class of racing. Basically the formula remains the same for the numerous varieties in interval programs:

A. A period of intense effort, followed by

B. A shorter period of rest or lesser effort,

C. Repeated again and again

To fully appreciate the effects of interval training you must understand the requirements of the racing cyclist as I see them:

1. **Cardio-Respiratory Fitness.** The foundation of basic ability for any sport is heart and lung conditioning. The more work these organs have to do, the more work they will be able to do, efficiency and strength coming from repeated efforts by the principle of overload. Heart and lungs must be worked as hard as possible during the training "work" interval, with the next work interval beginning just as soon as breathing and pulse rate return to a level that enables the exercise to be repeated at a good performance level.

2. **Strength.** Muscular strength is also best developed, in my opinion, by the principle of progressive overload. Again, the more you do the more you can do. Continual bursts of hard riding, within the gearing selected, are basic to interval training, and to the muscular "memory" which makes training seem like the racing for which it is intended to be a preparation. As I've said, no matter how you train, the races themselves are not run off under Long Slow Distance rules. LSD may give you the energy, but there should be a time in training when you do "get the feel" of going hard and fast. That's why there are few "pure LSD" advocates. Most of them do recommend a certain amount of speed work.

3. **Stamina.** Stamina—local muscular endurance—is achieved by repetition of the same movements. Unless there has been some correlation between the speed and patterns of actual racing with those in training, you will soon find your endurance factors insufficient for success.

4. **Speed.** The correlation of speed was referred to under Stamina. It is not difficult to imagine the problems of a rider who trains at 18 mph and then tries to race at a 25 mph average. No matter how fit he is, he will soon be in trou-

ble. He must practice at racing speeds. LSD advocates' speed sessions, again, are also done at race speed.

5. **Tolerance of Pain.** Successful cycle racing does not require you to become a masochist; you don't have to learn to love pain or anything like that. However, in a jam, on a climb, or in a long sprint the racer who can hang on and suffer that little bit longer, given equal levels of ability, usually emerges the winner. The location of your threshold of pain must be defined, and then that boundary must be pushed back. The winning racer is the one able to withstand acute discomfort, through knowing that he has felt the same pain numerous times in training and has willed his way past it. "Learn to suffer" should mean "Learn to overcome suffering."

OFF-SEASON TRAINING

If you live in an area where winter closes in tight, you might find that a few months of non-bike training such as working with weights, running, skiing or hiking do more long term good for your conditioning level then risking respiratory and muscular problems slogging your bike through snow and cold rains. Still, get back on your bike as early as you safely can, dressing for the weather and keeping your legs covered until absolutely sure of the conditions.

Start an early season training program using low gears, 69" through 73". Starting right in with a fixed gear at the beginning of your training program will develop good style, and insure that you keep working all the time. It seems hard to get US riders to acknowledge this, and if you must ride derailleur gears in the early phases of your training regimen keep to the low end and avoid dropping into high gears.

TABLE 1
EARLY SEASON TRAINING SCHEDULE

Week	Mon.	Tues.	Wed.	Thurs.	Fri.	Sat.	Sun.	Miles
1	20 S	20 F	30 G	10 F	20 S	30 S	50 G	170
2	20 S	15 F	30 F	10 F	20 S	30 S	50 G	175
3	20 S	25 F	30 G	15 F	20 S	30 S	50 G	180
4	20 S	20 F	20 G	15 F	20 S	30 S	60 G	185
5	20 S	20 F	30 G	15 F	20 S	30 S	60 G	195
6	20 S	20 F	30 G	20 F	20 S	30 S	60 G	200
7	20 S	20 F	30 G	20 F	30 G	30 S	60 G	210
8	20 S	20 F	30 G	20 F	30 G	30 S	70 G	220
9	20 S	20 F	30 G	20 F	30 G	30 S	70 G	220
10	20 S	20 F	30 G	20 F	30 G	20 S	Race (50)	190
11	20 S	20 F	30 G	20 F	30 G	10 S	Race (60)	190

TOTAL   2,135

(S = steady riding at about 20 mph; F = fast training, riding as hard as possible; G = group training, changing every 200-300 yards. Sunday group training should be done as a steady, non-stop ride carrying any food and drink that may be required.)

The Santa Monica Sunday morning "death ride" along the coastal highway is a Southern California off-season training tradition. I have ridden it in late December and watched some riders pushing gears of 100" or 103". They get a perverted pleasure out of making the intelligent rider who's out for training and not racing suffer, and when the racing season does arrive these big shot big gear pushers seem to be the first to get blown off the back of the packs. Nobody is supposed to "win" a training session or ride, but everyone participating is supposed to benefit by working together as a group.

Table No. 1 is a suggested early season road program for use before specializing in particular events. Remember, to me the "S" in the chart does not stand for "slow," it means "steady," and "F"—fast training means *an all-out effort that can be sustained over the distance.* The "G" group sessions, if you must train alone, can be done as repeated optimum output intervals; a good high speed group pace line where everyone pulls his proper turn at the front is a natural interval system.

SPECIALIZED TRAINING

At an early stage of my racing career in England I was fortunate to receive guidance from Norman Sheil, former world pursuit champion and British national coach and Olympic cycle team manager. Having won the Dunlop Cup, awarded annually to the best first season rider in the country, I was invited to attend the yearly training clinic at Lilleshall Hall conducted by Sheil. There it was possible to learn from the best, in classroom sessions, on the road, on the tracks, individually or riding with my contemporaries or with more experienced and established first raters.

TABLE 2

MAXIMUM PERFORMANCE PROGRAM: SPEED EVENTS

1. 6-12 months preparation training
2. 3-4 months intensive training period
3. Short training sessions—everyday, 1-2 hours/day; one day rest/week
4. One 3-4-hour session/week
5. 30-60 100% intervals/week
6. No hill work
7. 10 hours sleep/night, plus afternoon rest period
8. Balanced diet (milk, meats, vegetables, fresh fruit, bread, potatoes, etc.)

The actual styles of racing and training may have changed since then, but I believe that at Lilleshall I learned the basic requirements of a successful racing career. Beyond the tricks of the trade on the track or road, and the training schedules popular at the time, I think those clinics under Sheil's direction taught me self analysis and self discipline. An example of self analysis is keeping a complete racing and training diary. It isn't enough to just write up the total miles done each week, but keep track of all pertinent information for every race or ride. Your time, your gear, your placing, how you felt and perhaps (as I would do it)

TABLE 3

MAXIMUM PERFORMANCE PROGRAM: ENDURANCE EVENTS

1. 6-month *minimum* training period, 9-12 months preferred
2. Long training sessions every day (2-4 hours/day); one day of rest or light work per week.
3. One 5-6-hour session every other week.
4. High number of 80% intervals: 30-50 minutes per week
5. Hill work three times/week
6. 10 hours sleep/night, plus afternoon rest period
7. Balanced diet (milk, meats, vegetables, fresh fruit, bread, potatoes, etc.)

what sort of day it had been—wind, temperature, etc. Of course, record any changes made in saddle height and equipment so that you can look back and really know what difference they make.

The prime element of cycling self discipline is keeping to the program selected, riding the required miles in the manner called for by the schedule. Cheating on the training program can harm no one but yourself. I think that if you apply that self discipline you will find yourself better able to deal with the mental stresses of racing situations; you know you are physically ready as possible, and able to race with confidence. The one great exception is that if you are experiencing symptoms of overstress it's foolish to train. Stress symptoms are a physiological warning that your body has been given too much work.

Tables 2 through 5 represent four basic interval training programs based upon my training, experience and practice. Once again, these are not gospel, but suggestions. However, I do think of them as informed suggestions, better matched to racing requirements and human abilities than many others. They cover road and track programs, with the rider to select the program or programs that are directed toward the events he expects to ride.

TABLE 4

MAXIMUM ENDURANCE PROGRAM WITH GOOD SPEED

	Work (sec)	Rest (sec)	Repetition	Duration	Total Time
(1)	10	50	30	5 min.	½ hour
(2)	10	50	60	10 min.	1 hour
(3)	20	100	15	5 min.	½ hour
(4)	20	100	30	10 min.	1 hour
(5)	30	150	10	5 min.	½ hour
(6)	30	150	20	10 min.	1 hour
(7)	30	150	30	15 min.	1½ hour

80% effort, which means pulse rate 160-180 at end of work phase

THE SPRINT

My track specialties were the kilometer and the sprints. Both require speed and endurance. Therefore, my own training progran encompassed both short and long intervals (see tables 2 and 3). Additionally, twice per week I met with other sprint specialists for track workouts with the emphasis being applied to leadout sprints.

Leadout training is an excellent group technique for improving speed. Riders should ride in line in groups of three or four racers of equal ability, with the leading rider winding up the pace at 500 meters and jumping to attain maximum speed at the 300-meter mark. His effort should be flat out, enabling the riders "Sitting on" to take advantage of the slipstreaming phenomenon to come around at the appropriate time, usually in the last 50 meters. Times taken at the 200-meter mark for the second placed rider under this training system often exceed those attained during competition.

There is a common hangup about being beaten, even in training, that results in wasted effort. Some riders when in the lead position are more concerned with conserving energy for the final yards than in helping their training partners to improve. They simply must "win" from the front instead of giving their all in a maximum-effort leadout. It is a common ego trip, and a good coach should give any rider guilty of doing this the sort of verbal "boot in the saddle" I received when I "won" a leadout training sprint from the front.

TABLE 5

MAXIMUM SPEED PROGRAM, WITH SMALL AMOUNT OF ENDURANCE

	Work 100%	Rest	Repetition	Duration	Total Time
(1)	10 sec.	110	10	1 min. 40 sec.	20 min.
(2)	10 sec.	170	20	3 min. 20 sec.	1 hr.
(3)	15 sec.	105	10	2 min. 30 sec.	20 min.
(4)	15 sec.	105	20	5 min.	1 hr.

100% effort—pulse higher than 180, preferably near 200

In the immediate period before major competitions such as National or World Championships extra long leadouts behind a motor should be included. The Derny machine, ideal for track use, is a motor-assisted pacing bicycle of French origin. It is highly geared and capable of good speeds and a very smooth pace—something very important to the rider who will be sitting only fractions of an inch behind the machine. Aside from its training use the Derny is often used for motorpaced racing on European indoor tracks and for the final leg of the Bordeaux-Paris 365-mile nonstop classic race. A low-horsepower motorcycle makes a fair replacement for a Derny. Use a model under 250cc, large enough for the required speed but not too large for sensitive control and smooth acceleration.

Working behind a motor is excellent speed training, but the extra long lead-outs of 800 meters at maximum speed behind the machine and then coming around it for an additional 200-meter sprint were pure murder!

During track training sessions many riders completely ignore working on their command of sprint tactics. They do their miles and their jumps mechanically, without exercising the mind to the point where not only can the right move be made, but it will be made instinctively. In my opinion, given a fair state of training the most important part of being a successful sprinter is tactical competence. Tactics must be considered part of your workout and practiced with the same devotion given to the more physical aspects.

The start of my own tactical workouts would be a series of jumps, first rolling slowly, and then at a mentally set time, accelerating to maximum speed over the shortest possible distance. Pick two spots on the track approximately 50 meters apart for a start and finish. Of course, this can be made more interesting in groups of three or four riders. You may compare performances and pick up some ideas about their styles and abilities.

For training in sprint maneuvers it is necessary to work in pairs, and a partner of equal caliber should be selected. The pair should alternate positions for all the maneuvers, working at "opponent control" from the front, with both high on the banking, pinning him to the fence, keeping him nailed there if he tries to slow down and get out of the box. This is a tactic best employed on fairly steeply banked tracks such as Encino, Portland and Detroit.

Time should also be spent on controlling your opponent from the front at speed, over the last 200 meters. Remember, as long as you have not entered the pole position you have the whole width of the track at your disposal. Use it. Keeping a racer on your hip until the last 150 meters and then diving off of the banking will make it almost impossible for him to come around you for a win. Even after you go below the safety line a couple of friendly hooks, all within the pole position, moving sharply from the bottom to the top of the pole, will often be enough to send your opponent wide and break his concentration.

It is strategy, not simple power, that should govern the timing of your initial jump. Ideally it should take your opponent by surprise. In riding from the rear position I won many races by learning and taking advantage of the other racer's pattern of head movements—when he watched me and when he watched the track. I could time my jump at the exact moment he turned his head forward. The split second gained over his reaction time sometimes made the difference between winning and losing.

Another useful ploy to learn is crank positioning. This can be employed from the front or the back. Most riders have their most effective jump with the initial thrust coming from their right leg. The time for you to go, then, is when his left leg is in the upper position, preferably in the "dead spot" 11 o'clock position. Again, this should become a reflexive, automatic element of your race tactics and must be practiced like any other move.

Many riders are of the single-minded sort. They become keyed up during competition and narrow their concentration to the task at hand. Sometimes a "looser" rider can psych out one of these racing "machines" with small talk and innuendos during the match. It isn't against the rules, but will not earn you any "most popular racer" awards. Psychology is an important racing tool; learn to use it offensively and defensively.

In the sprints the rear rider has the element of surprise going for him. Learn how to keep the rearward position if you want it. Take training time to learn the art of balancing, especially in the corners on steep bankings. Most racers have trouble controlling a balance on a steep bank, and advantage can be taken there by forcing the other man to the front. It is important in a stand-still to always have your bicycle facing down the banking if it is necessary to move out in a hurry. Sounds elementary, but I have watched nationally ranked sprinters facing their bikes up the banking in this situation and saw them left standing when their opponent rode off.

The finishing "throw"—thrusting the bike forward across the line—should also be practiced. In my racing career I was known for that maneuver. It won me many races, not only from the long, searing, desperate inches gained that way, but also by luring my opponent into a false security. Many times when coming around the outside in the second position I would seem to be struggling hard just to hold on, not gaining the added distance needed to come around. The other racer would be convinced that it was unnecessary to dig into his physical reserves for a second kick. Just before the finish line I would throw my bike forward for the inches needed for victory. It often worked, and even worked more than once on riders who should have learned better. The "throw" has to be used with caution; control can easily be lost. In the final of the 1971 US Grand Prix I made a desperate effort to beat Skip Cutting, American Olympic sprinter, and lost my bike, crashing heavily into the banking. A more dramatic finish than I wished.

1,000 METER TIME TRIAL

Since the kilometer is an all-out effort from the start, most riders consider it to be the most grueling of the track events. A top kilo rider must be acutely aware of his individual capabilities and balance his efforts throughout the event. Many riders expend so much effort in the first 500 meters that they do not have strength to maintain the speed over the full distance. Intervals over 250 and 500 meters (table 4) will teach you to pace yourself, and soon you will know the difference between a 16-second or 17-second 250 meters. Give special importance to perfecting your start. Valuable time can be gained by a fast, straight start, keeping as close as possible to the bottom pole line.

The kilo takes an enormous amount of mental effort and while positioned on the starting line, deep breathing exercises will calm the mind and insure that your lungs are full of fresh oxygen for this demanding event. Heed Tim Mountford's remarks about the confidence gained from good basic fitness. Assume your riding position and await the starter's orders.

You must learn to attain your maximum speed between 100 and 150 meters from the gun out of the saddle, then sit down smoothly and maintain your effort throughout. The final 300 meters become extremely difficult and it is at this point that the race can be won or lost. Special effort should be made to maintain your form and not to be fighting your bike.

Concentrate on overcoming the pain that your body is suffering. It is my belief that the racer that can endure the most suffering will generally be the winner. It is really a question of self-discipline; the mind can make the body go past the point where you feel you must slack off, and do it without damage. So perfect your starts, learn to judge your speed over the first 700 meters, and suffer through to the finish. At all times concentrate on riding close to the lower pole line to ensure going the shortest distance.

Specialists in the kilo generally use 24- or 28-spoked wheels, depending on weight and riding styles. These wheels are not normally used in training, but shortly before a big event work out once or twice on your racing wheels. The lighter wheels have vastly different handling characteristics; it is important that the difference not come as a surprise to you during competition.

PURSUIT

As mentioned, my own specialties were the sprint and the kilo, and I thought myself unqualified to give chapter and verse regarding pursuit training and tactics. For this I sought the aid of my friend Ron Skarin, Olympic pursuitist.

Ron's own approach is that pursuit training should be essentially the same as that of a road racer—that is, motor pacing, intervals, plenty of hills and competing in all types of road races. A month prior to national or world class competition his training takes on a more specialized form. Hills are eliminated from his workouts and more concentration is paid to track training in two or three sessions per week.

Three weeks before the competition Skarin increases his interval training program and uses motor pacing to increase his speed. All workouts are on heavy wheels and tubulars, with a gear ratio two inches lower than he will ride in competition. This program is continued up to a week before the event; then he reduces his road training to two sessions of approximately 40 miles each in a low gear with good leg spin. During track workouts intervals will be significantly reduced, with the training time and effort invested in working in pace lines or behind the motor, with special attention paid to not exhausting himself physically or mentally. On the day of the race Skarin does an easy track warmup of about five to 10 miles, not pushing himself. He then returns to the track center, cleans up and puts on fresh clothing for the event. Just before his race he spends 10 minutes working out on the rollers. This loosens him up and increases his pulse rate.

At the starting line, as in the kilo, special attention is given to hyperventilation—good for the nerves and insures a good intake of fresh oxygen. In a pursuit your first ride of a series will usually be a time trial to establish seeding and the pairing for the subsequent rounds. Unlike some of the world's leading pursuiters Ron does not ride to a pre-selected time or for a specific placing in the seeding ladder.

Skarin says he thinks it important to pace yourself to a 95% effort in the first 1000 meters, making sure not to overextend yourself, risking a "blow up" later in the ride. However, when "riding the man" in the actual matches, he must keep alert that his opponent does not take a flyer in the early stages of the pursuit. Conversely, if he finds himself gaining rapidly on his competitor he makes a point of not becoming over eager and increasing his pace to catch his man. This is a common problem with pursuiters: Getting their man in their sights early in the match and then blowing up in an effort to bridge that tantalizing gap. The result often is a shattered program, no sustaining rhythm and being ground down by your opponent's steady pace.

Ron considers the second and third 1000 meters to be the most mentally demanding part of the pursuit. At that stage careful concentration should be given to breathing and maintaining a steady 95% effort. Going into the last 1000 meters the pace should be gradually increased until the bell lap. Then your body should be functioning at 99% effort through to the finish. Of course race through the finish line, not just to it!

MADISON RACING

The Madison is a six-day event which enjoyed tremendous US popularity in the early 1900's. It was named after Madison Square Garden, New York, which was the mecca of cycling during that era. Almost all major cities in the states had indoor tracks, but since the war little interest has been shown by Americans and consequently this facet of the sport is now promoted almost solely in European countries. The event is a race of teams usually comprised of two men but occasionally three. Each team races in relay fashion with one rider from each team participating at all times. Each rider will ride one or two laps and then relay his partner into the race with a handsling or a hefty tug of the shorts (a "jamming tool" should be inserted). Throughout the six-day race there will be many other events in which points are awarded—point races, devil takes the hindmost, etc.

The winner of the overall event will be the team which covers the greatest number of laps. However, in the event of two or more teams having the same lap placings positions will be determined on a point standing.

Many race promoters now include a one-hour or two-hour Madison to conclude the race program. This style of racing is spectacular and is enjoying increased popularity in the United States.

HANDICAP RACES

Handicap races are generally contended over distances between ¼ and 1 mile. These races are very popular in England, Denmark and Australia. Start positions are determined from previous race performances, with the national champion generally starting in the scratch position.

DEVIL TAKE THE HINDMOST

This race is often referred to in the US as a miss-and-out, but in essence is an elimination event. Generally the last rider crossing the start/finish line each lap is eliminated until the predetermined number of riders remain. This is usually three riders who will then sprint the final lap for the official placings. This event is a real crowd pleaser with tightly bunched sprints every lap.

UNKNOWN DISTANCE

This is precisely what the name suggests, a massed-start event in which the final lap is signified by the bell at which time the riders participate in a "battle royal" for the final honors.

POINTS RACING

Victory in this event is awarded to the rider amassing the highest number of total points and not to the winner of the final sprint. Points are awarded generally 5-3-2-1 to the four top riders in numerous intermediate sprints. The last lap usually carries double points and it is therefore necessary for each rider to be aware of the others' point standings since the last lap can often change the race result.

TRACK DISCIPLINE

Track discipline and courtesy are of fundamental importance. Our sport is not without its physical hazards. I can testify to that! When the metal pin that held my hip together after my fall in Portland finally was removed, I had it mounted on a plaque in my office wall with the engraved legend, "Munchen 1972" as sort of a black joke. However, those are rare results involving some minor chances of risk in the course of a match or race.

What is infuriating is the frequent reports of training injuries at the tracks. Many riders seem to amble along in training on the track as if they were on a club social ride, showing no regard for racers working on their own individual training programs. Work to the following guidelines until they become instinctive. They are for your protection as well as the other fellow's:

● Thoroughly check your equipment before going on the track. Are your tubulars securely attached to the rims? How is your chain tension? Are wheel nuts tight; handlebars secure in the frame, etc.?

● Put on your crash hat before mounting the track, not while riding around.

● Watch carefully not to impede other riders when you roll off, and just as soon as you have sufficient momentum move up the track banking out of the way of the pace line riders.

● When riding in a pace line or training in the pole position never swing up the track without first checking for riders moving around the outside of the pace line.

● At all times keep both hands on the bars, preferably in the hooks. Save the victory salute of two upstretched arms for your first national championship!

4

Meet
The Racer

In early November, 1974, we mailed questionnaires to 60 of the top racing cyclists, asking them about their training, racing and dietary habits and personal opinions on subjects related to bike racing. We got replies from 28 cyclists—22 category I senior class riders, three top juniors, two women and one veteran. There were 11 riders from the East Coast, seven from the West Coast, five from the Midwest and five from the South.

Three 1974 national champions sent back questionnaires, as did seven ex-national champions. Eight current state champions and at least three ex-state champions answered. At least seven of the riders have ridden in national jerseys at the world championships or other international events. All of the other riders to whom we sent the questionnaire had frequently placed in the top three in their races.

JOHN C. ALLIS

PERSONAL: 32, 5'8", 152 lbs. 14 years in racing, prior sports: soccer, skiing, mountain climbing.

RACING: Best races: '74 National Road Champion; 16th, 1300-mi. 15-day '71 Tour of Mexico; 2nd 1968 1100-mi. 11-day Tour de la Nouvelle France; 1st '64 190-km. Paris-Cayeux sur Mer. Bikes raced: Raleigh Pro/Raleigh Team. Events: crit., 4000-m indiv. & team pursuit, road, stage, time trials. Favorite type: stage races. Preferred distance: 100+ miles.

TRAINING: Early season miles (beginning and just before season starts): 300-400. Mid-season miles: 300-400. No intervals, trains 90% alone, 10% in group, 90% LSD, 10% unspecified. No special preparation before races, 20-40 miles day before. No weight training. Warmup 15 minutes minimum roll before race. Important qualities: aggressiveness, endurance, determination. No training diary ("Did keep miles/pulse/weight in 1968.") Guidelines for training: "Just have to know yourself." Winter layoff four months, skiing, hiking, etc. Winter mileage: low. Learned tactics and riding in a bunch by training. Never experiments with equipment changes.

DIET: Never does carbo-loading, never fasts, no special pre-race diet. During races eats fruit (especially bananas and pears), tea and honey every 15 minutes to half hour after two hours. Takes multivitamins during stage races and vitamin C at other times. Eats no greasy foods and a balanced diet.
REASONS IN SPORT: "I love the racing."

LES BARCZEWSKI

PERSONAL: 17, 5'7", 150 lbs. Five years in racing, prior sports: speed skating, swimming.

RACING: Best races: '74 Junior European Championships 5th in sprint; '70-'72 National Intermediate Road Champion; '71-'72 National Intermediate Track Champion. Bikes raced: RRB Custom, Masi, Paramount. Events: criterium, sprints, scratch, road. Favorite type: sprint.

TRAINING: Mileage unspecified. Trains 50% alone, 50% in group, 90% LSD, 10% intervals. Trains with weights, unspecified. Warms up "until I feel loose." Important qualities: aggressiveness, psych. Keeps training diary, enters miles, type of training, times, conditions. Guidelines for training: performance results. Winter layoff 6-7 months, speed skating. Winter mileage: 0. Learned tactics by "talking it over." Never experiments with equipment change.

DIET: Never carbo-loads. Never fasts. Pre-race diet: eggs the day of the race "because it's my favorite." During criteriums drinks "whatever feels the best." No supplements.

REASON IN SPORT: "Because I like racing very much, and I enjoy the people associated with this sport."

DEL BLUNDELL

PERSONAL: 19, 6'1", 170 lbs. 2½ years in racing, prior sports: football, basketball, etc.

RACING: Best races: La Boucherie Criterium '73, 1st place; Tour de Loui-siana 3rd overall, 1st in criterium stage. Bikes raced: Cooper for track, Eisentraut for road. Events: all. Favorite type: stage. Preferred distance: 100 miles.

TRAINING: Early season miles: 175-200 easy road miles, Jan. and Feb. Mid-season miles: 200-400, 500 maximum. Does intervals: 1 min. on, 1 off alternating big and little gears five times. Trains 50% alone and 50% in group, 90% LSD, 5% intervals, some motorpacing. Special preparation before races: rides 25-40 miles day before. No weight training. Warms up five miles "medium effort." Important qualities: aggressiveness. Keeps training diary, enters miles, course, weight, pulse, other notes. Training guidelines: "If pulse is unusually high I just ride short and easy. Winter layoff 4 weeks, running and playing basketball, Winter mileage: 175. Learned tactics, riding in a bunch by riding club races. Never experiments with equipment changes (except to adjust position).

DIET: Does carbo-loading for every race. Never fasts. Special pre-race diets: carbohydrates two days before race, extra proteins while training. During races eats "whatever I get a chance to in long races, eat about two hours before a short race." Takes vitamins C and E, wheat germ oil and salt. Other factors: "Just no junk!"

REASONS IN SPORT: "I am an active person and other sports like football, soccer, etc. are too hard on the body. There's no feeling like being super-fit!"

DAN BROWN

PERSONAL: 21, 6'0", 180 lbs. Six years in racing, prior sports: skiing, water skiing.

RACING: Best races: Junior National Road Race 1970, 4th; Mt. Hamilton race 1st junior; Northern Calif. Junior Road Champion '71; Northern Calif. Senior Track 10-mile '72, 2nd place. Bikes raced: Masi, Velo Sport. Events: Criterium, track, stage, time trials. Favorite type: criterium. Preferred distance: 30 miles.

TRAINING: Early season miles: 200-300. Mid-season miles: 200-300. Does intervals: sprints with full recovery and jams with incomplete recovery. Trains 50% alone, 50% in group, 60% LSD, 10% faster than race pace, 15% intervals, 15% race pace. Special preparation before races: rest 1½ days before, concentrate on type of riding required in the event. Uses weights: arms, back and shoulders; pull-back and upstroke of pedal motion. Warms up 1-3 miles at medium pace before race. Important qualities: brains, good general conditioning. Keeps training diary, enters: miles, time, exercises for day, week, month and year. Trains by awareness of stress factors, awareness of race speed decrease. Winter layoff 4-5 months, skiing. Winter mileage: 35 miles per week. Learned tactics, riding in bunch, "from friends and personal experience."

DIET: Uses carbo-loading, no details. Never fasts, no special pre-race diets. Drinks "a little in short races, eat once or twice in long races." No supplements.

REASONS IN SPORT: "Like to win."

PIERRE CHARES

PERSONAL: 34, 5'11", 150 lbs. Fifteen years in racing, prior sports: high school track and field.

RACING: Best races: New York state road champion '73; '73 Atala Grand Prix, 1st; '72 Century Road Club Assoc. 50-mi., 1st; Gablinger Beery Trophy, 1st. Bikes raced: Limongi custom. Events: criterium, madison, road, cyclo-x, stage races, time trials. Favorite type: road. Preferred distance: over 100 kilometers (62.4 mi.).

TRAINING: Early season miles: 170 varying with weather. Mid-season miles: 200-300 depending on feelings. Does intervals: "on short rides 25-30 miles will go steady one way 20 mph and return sprinting at road signs. Also will attend jam sessions on track with group of other riders—training consisting of

1974 National Road Champion John Allis leads at the Walpole, Mass. Criterium in the summer of '74. (R. George for Cyclenews

pace line followed by fast and furious team races (once a week only). Trains 50% alone, 50% in group, "mostly LSD with track and sprint injected between." Special preparation before races: "usually layoff day prior to race and day after race and sometimes will take off somewhere in between for other rest days. I ride four days a week which includes the race." No weight training. Warms up 5-10 miles depending on time available before a race. Important qualities: endurance, speed. Training diary previously included miles, how and with whom covered. Guidelines for training: "Have learned through years of my capability to recuperate from a race or training effort, so I force rest days on myself." Winter layoff "until snow," x-country skiing, roller training, some running "to keep lungs and endocrine glands prepared for abrupt strain." Winter miles inconsistent "due to weather—about 30 miles daily and a bit more on weekends." Learned tactics and riding in a bunch "from experienced riders, racing in Belgium in '62 and in races. Never experiments with equipment changes.

DIET: Never does carbo-loading, never fasts. Special pre-race diet: "carbohydrates such as noodles, mixed with meats and vegetables." During short race uses "ERG, rice cake loaded with raisins for potassium, pineapple chunks, etc. In races over 50 miles, ERG." No supplements ("I find I do as well without.") "I use Hoffman's Super Gain Weight High Protein blended with milk daily to maintain my good racing weight."

REASON IN SPORT: "Glory. Fitness. It's become an addiction. I am fascinated by the bike, its speed and also the competition."

LINDSAY CRAWFORD

PERSONAL: 34, 6'3", 180 lbs. Five years in racing, prior sports experience unspecified.

RACING: Best races: '71 Tour of California, 2nd place team; '72 Italian Swiss Colony Time Trials, 15 1st places; '73 Napa 50-mi. Time Trial, 1st; '74 California State Road Champion; '74 Tour of Marin, 1st. Bikes raced: Eisentraut, Cinelli, Paramount. Events: criterium, pursuit, road, stage races, time trials. Favorite type: stage races. Preferred distance: 90-125 miles.

TRAINING: Early season miles: Jan-Feb. 300, Mar.-May 350. Mid-season miles: June-July 350-400 including races. Does some intervals, type unspecified. Trains 95% alone, 5% in group, 75% LSD, 5% intervals, 5% long hard distance, 15% motor pacing. Special preparation before races: "Don't believe in not riding day before race—like to ride 25-40 easy miles day before." Trains with weights: mainly during winter with fairly light weights and numerous repetitions. Warms up 5-8 miles at an easy pace or rides to race if it's not more than 30 miles. Keeps a training diary, enters miles, weight training, race results, body weight. Trains by awareness of stress factors. Winter layoff 6-8 weeks, skiing just for recreation. Winter mileage 100. Learned tactics, riding in a bunch from "trial and error— had virtually no coaching." Never experiments with equipment changes.

DIET: Uses carbo-loading "only for special events—don't think it's possible to always carbo load when racing two or three times a week." Never fasts. Special pre-race diet: "Try to always maintain a good diet—no hard-to-digest foods. Keep a higher than normal carbohydrate intake but not in the form of "junk' food." During a race eats "usually only water for short races—fruit, sometimes cookies, water or ERG for longer events. Always eat before hungry." Vitamin supplements—especially B, C and E and calcium. Avoids candy, soft drinks, greasy and fried foods. "Must maintain high caloric intake during season and feel that it should be in form of good nutritious food."

REASON IN SPORT: "It's a good feeling to be fit and also to demonstrate your fitness by performing well in racing. Of course there's no feeling like riding a race against the best and winning."

MATT CRISTE

PERSONAL: 25, 6'4", 192 lbs. Three years in racing, prior sports: skeet shooting, motorcycle racing, competitive fencing, others.

RACING: '72 Sacramento Criterium, 9th place; '73 Northern California Track Champion at 1000 meters; Pedali Alpini Twilight Series winner. Bikes raced: Bob Jackson, Holdsworth, Masi, Paramount, De Rosa, home-built. Events: kilometer, 10-mile, sprints, road. Favorite type: madison, track events. Preferred distance: 40 miles

TRAINING: Early season miles: 200—long club rides, short rides on 65" fixed gear with three or more riders. Mid-season miles: more fixed-gear rides approximately 25 miles in length, five sprints at fast pace. Motor pacing, short time trials, fast pace lines, intervals. Does intervals: approximately ½-mile on road bike, large and small gears, two sets of five. Trains 10% alone, 90% in group, 20% LSD, 10% race pace, 20% intervals, 40% race pace, 10% practicing jumps, leadouts, etc. Special preparation before races: "If Sunday is race day, Thursday is last hard day. Friday a moderate speed ride with three sprints, Saturday fixed-gear easy, with two sprints." Uses weights: "pre-season entire body first, then mostly legs." Warms up "approximately 20% of ride length, fast enough to draft." Important qualities: aggressiveness, determination, self-knowledge, speed, intelligence. Keeps a training diary, enters heart and breath rates, miles and pace and type of ride. Guidelines for training: notes "speed over distance improvement, time trial times, gears I can push." Winter layoff three months, football, jogging, weight training. Winter mileage: 50. Learned tactics, riding in a bunch "from motorcycle racing, reading, verbal orientation, riding with my eyes open!" Experiments with equipment changes: "I'm sure my bike was never the same twice."

DIET: uses carbo-loading "every race if possible," never fasts. Special pre-race diet is carbo-loading. During races: "Short race, water, orange slices; long race—water, orange slices, cookies and other carbohydrates." Supplements: vitamins C and E, wheat germ oil, B complex. Eats "lots of vegetables out of my own garden, no over-processed foods, high protein, etc."

REASONS IN SPORT: "Strong romance with two-wheel competition, identity formation and reinforcement, prestige, health, meet new people, anti-smog, etc."

STEPHEN DAYTON

PERSONAL: 23, 6'0", 155 lbs. Seven years in racing, prior sports: cross-country, baseball, basketball.

RACING: Best races: '71 National Road Champion; '68 National Junior Road Race, 3rd place; Indiana State Road Champion '68-'71, '74. Bikes raced: Legnano, Teledyne, Hi-E. Events: criterium, road, stage races. Favorite type: criterium. Preferred distance: 50 miles.

TRAINING: Early season miles: 60-100. Mid-season miles: 60-200. Does intervals: ½-mile, 90-second rest—start with three, work up to eight every other day. Trains 15% alone, 85% in group, 10% LSD, 10% faster than race pace, 15% intervals, 25% race pace, 30% long hard distance, 10% sprints. Special preparations before races: layoff day before if it's a big race. Never uses weights. Warms up 4-5 miles at 15 mph in low gear. Important qualities: experience, endurance, sprint. Doesn't keep a training diary. Trains by awareness of stress factors. Winter layoff two months. Winter mileage 60. Learned tactics, riding in a bunch "from other racers in area (weekly club races)." Experiments "primarily with different tires and rims and lighter components."

DIET: Never carbo-loads, never fasts. Special pre-race diet: pancakes, or french toast, waffles (no milk. During race "drink Gatorade, eat fruit—bananas, oranges, peaches). Drink one bottle in first 50 miles, two bottles each 50 miles thereafter.

REASONS IN SPORT: "Enjoy bike riding and racing gives me incentive to train and stay in shape."

MICHAEL FRAYSSE

PERSONAL: 30, 5'10", 160 lbs. Twenty-three years in racing, prior sports: cross-country (state champion), speed skating (2nd twice in nationals), five college letters in football and track.

RACING: Best races: National Track Championships, third twice; six times New Jersey state champion; member of US cycling team at World Championships. "Placed in every major open race on East Coast during my career. Bikes raced: Paris-Sport road, Lemongi track. Events: criterium, all track events, road, cyclo-x, stage races, time trials. Favorite type: criterium and track events.

TRAINING: Early season miles: 200. Mid-season miles: 200, 100 racing. Never does intervals. Trains 100% in group, 25% LSD, 10% faster than race pace, 25% race pace, 25% long hard distance, 15% on track. Special preparation before races: "nothing day before, easy two days before." Never uses weights, warmup "varies with the event, the shorter the race the more warmup is necessary." Important qualities: "All." Doesn't keep a training diary. Training guidelines: "I know myself and how I feel best." Winter layoff two months, ice skating. Winter mileage unspecified. Learned tactics, riding in a bunch "by good coaching and experience doing it." Never experiments with equipment changes: "There is no need—the equipment is not as important as most riders think."

DIET: Uses carbo-loading last four days before every race, never fasts. Special pre-race diet: low protein. During races diet "depends on temperature. The higher the temperature the more liquid required." Takes vitamin E 600 mg., vitamin C 600 i.u., salt.

REASONS IN SPORT: "Glory, fitness. My grandfather and father both were on Olympic teams and coached. My grandfather was five times president of the ABL and coached the 1928 and '32 Olympic teams. I have managed the last four world teams and coached two."

BILL GUAZZO

PERSONAL: 26, 6'0", 165 lbs. Eight years in racing, prior sports: high school and college football, swimming.

RACING: Best races: '72 Fitchburg 50-mile, 2nd; '72 Cross-Florida, 2nd; '71 West Rock Road Race, 1st; Connecticut Road Champion '68, '71, '73. Bikes raced: Raleigh RRA and Witcomb. Events: criterium, road, cyclo-x, stage races, time trials. Favorite type: road. Preferred distance: 100 kilometers and up.

TRAINING: Early season miles: "Jan.-March alternate running, lifting weights, then start more miles, especially on weekends. In March taper off lifting weights and do more miles, building up to 200-300 miles a week before the season starts." Mid-season miles: "I usually race to a point on Sunday where a Monday workout is worthless, being too tired. Tuesday—intervals or time trial. Wednesday—LSD. Thursday—long fast distance. Friday—intervals. Saturday—rest or race. Does intervals "once or twice a week—45 seconds at 90%, one minute rest, and repeat 12 times." Trains 90% alone, 10% in group, 20% LSD, 10% intervals, 40% race pace, 30% long hard distance. Special preparation before races: "Day off before or easy 10 miles is usually enough to recover from any training." "Weight training in winter consists of three times a week on Universal Gym—leg presses with max. weights, 2-3 sets of 10-12 repetitions; leg extensions: three sets of 15 with max. weight. Triceps extensions, situps, pushups." Warms up five miles steady before race. Important qualities: "aggressiveness, jump, recovery, time trialing at end, endurance." Doesn't keep a training diary but plans workouts weekly. Training guidelines: "The more it hurts, the better it must be for me. Winter layoff one month, running, cyclo-x, will try x-country skiing this year. Winter mileage varies. Learned tactics, riding in a bunch by "trial and error." Never experiments with equipment changes: "Set it up at the beginning of the season and it stays pretty much that way, all year."

DIET: Uses carbo-loading weekly, never fasts. Special pre-race diet: liver meal two days before, carbohydrates day before. During races "up to 50 miles, depending on heat, up to one bottle; over 50 I try to eat every half-hour." Takes vitamin C, wheat germ oil, salt, dessicated liver, brewer's yeast. Eats lots of granola, yogurt, no fried foods.

REASONS IN SPORT: "First I enjoy riding a bike, enjoy riding with a bunch of other guys enjoying themselves. I've been at it long enough that I don't worry about the races that much. If I do well fine, if not ok. I'm having fun (fun suffering??)."

GREGG HOWE

PERSONAL: 26, 5'7", 135 lbs. Four years in racing, prior sports: high school and college basketball.

RACING: Best races: '74 Aspen Alpine Cup, 11th; '73 Tour of Baja, in 20s. Bike raced: Frejus. Events: criterium, road, stage races, time trials. Favor-

ite type: stage races. Preferred distance: over 80 miles.
TRAINING: Early season miles: 200. Mid-season miles: up to 400 for important races. Does intervals "Before important races—30 seconds rest/go." Trains 5% maximum alone, over 95% in group, 10% LSD, 30% faster than race pace, 5% intervals, 45% race pace, 10% long hard distance. Uses weights in a "short winter program to strengthen back." Warms up 2-4 miles slow for any riding. Important qualities: presence of mind, endurance. Keeps a training diary, enters: miles, pulse in morning, competitive standing among club riders. Training guidelines: race performance. Winter layoff three weeks. Winter mileage: 200. Learned tactics, riding in a bunch on club rides. Doesn't make equipment changes.

DIET: Carbo-loading, fasting unspecified. Special pre-race diet: "large meals, but easily digestible." During races uses "water laced with lemon and dextrose during late stages, nothing under 60 miles; fruit for longer races." No supplements.

REASONS IN SPORT: "Sense of community enterprise with club members, physical well-being."

JIM HUNTER

PERSONAL: 24, 6'0", 160 lbs. Thirteen years in racing, prior sports: basketball, football.

RACING: Best races: '72-'73 Quebec-Montreal road race, 3rd, 2nd; '70 World Championships, finished in first lead group; '74 Tour of Ireland; "'74 will be a Raleigh pro!" Bikes raced: Masi, Colnago Super. Events: criterium, track team and six-day, road, stage races. Favorite type: road or criterium. Preferred distance: "over 100 miles with a very demanding course. I feel the tougher the race, the better I'll do."

TRAINING: Early season miles: "as much as possible." Mid-season miles: "an average of 65 miles per day—400-600 per week, with 100 to 160 miles on the weekends. Doesn't do intervals but "motorpace twice a week 40-50 miles at 30-35 mph. Trains "only and always with just one other rider, my coach." 40% LSD, 10% faster than race pace, 10% intervals, 15% race pace, 25% long hard distance. Special preparation before races: "In season, usually just a short ride the day before the race, usually 20 miles. The type of race determines my week of training. Uses weights in winter "until I can ride every day, usually March 1." Warms up for a race "usually about 20 minutes—in Europe, though, it was a lot longer." Important qualities: "*aggressiveness*—you must attack and go with the right breaks." Keeps a training diary, enters distance, time, type of training, weekly total of miles. Training guidelines: "I personally can feel myself come up to a peak and then level off. This comes, I think, through experience." Winter layoff one month, "x-country skiing, skating, running and just keeping active." Winter mileage: Jan.-Mar. average 30 miles a ride depending on weather. Learned tactics, riding in a bunch "by riding in good races and keeping my mouth shut and ears open and watching and learning something new every race. I still do this now, watching other good riders and seeing what they are doing, etc." Never experiments with equipment changes, "but I am very fussy about it—I always go with the best—Campagnolo Super Record, Clement tires, etc."

DIET: Uses carbo-loading but frequency unknown, never fasts. Special pre-race diet: "morning of race, cheese omelette, pancakes, oatmeal, toast, honey, tea. During race,"depending on the race and weather usually either water, tea, fruit punch and eat oranges, etc. If you eat right the morning of the race you don't need to eat too much in the race. Supplements: B_{12}, C, wheat germ, E.

REASONS IN SPORT: "I love competition and have to compete and be good at something. Whatever I do, I want to do well and give it everything I have. There is nothing better or more satisfying than winning."

JIM KEOGH

PERSONAL: 38, 5'8", 150 lbs. Sixteen years in racing, prior sports: swimming, tennis, running.

RACING: Best races: '70 German 100, 1st; '74 Princeton Invitational, 3rd; '70 Essex Co, 1st; '70 Lake Canadaigua, 4th. Bikes raced: Frejus, Rolls, Pennine. Events: all. Favorite type: stage races. Preferred distance: 75-80 miles.

TRAINING: Early season miles: 250-300. 1000 miles in 66-inch gear, then up to the '70's later. Mid-season miles: 200-250 in 42 x 15—53 x 14, "a new type of training which (US professional rider Jackie) Simes and I do—tempo training." No longer does intervals. Trains mostly alone or in group of two, 10% LSD, 10% faster than race pace, 10% race pace, tempo training and fast pedaling. Special preparation before races: "two days before, slow rides at 15 mph for 25-30 miles." Very little weight training. Warms up about five miles "snappy low gear for road events." Important qualities: aggressiveness. Doesn't keep training diary. Training guidelines: "I don't ride Monday or Friday and sleep one extra hour on these days. No winter layoff, does snow games, skating, etc., in winter. Winter mileage: 100. Learned tactics, riding in a bunch by experience. Never experiments with equipment changes.

DIET: Uses carbo-loading, frequency unspecified, never fasts. Special pre-race diet: "General food plus maccaroni, bread, cake." During race, orange juice, water, rice water, oranges, bananas, bread and jam. Takes B-complex plus iron. Eats "a lot of salads during the week."

REASONS IN SPORT: "A little bit of everything, a feeling of freedom."

FRANÇOIS MERTENS

PERSONAL: 42, 6'0", 160 lbs. Twenty-five years in racing, prior sports: soccer.

RACING: Best races: seven times New York State Champion; winner Sommerville Classic; three times National Best All-Round; winner Eastern Prestige standings once. Bikes raced: Belgian-made lugless cycles. Events: criterium, track, road, stage races. Favorite type: all. Preferred distance: 100+ miles.

TRAINING: Early season miles: 100. Mid-season miles: 200. Does no intervals. Trains 100% alone, 90% LSD, 10% race pace. No special preparation before races, no weights, no warmup. Important qualities: race intellect. No training diary. Training guidelines: "Do not ride when fatigued." Winter layoff six months, no winter sports, no mileage in winter. Learned tactics, riding in bunch by observing. Never experiments with equipment changes.

DIET: No carbo-loading, fasting, special pre-race diet. During race, takes tea and Coke syrup, eats only in beginning of road races, "in stage races eat continuously."

REASONS IN SPORT: "Love of competition."

DAVID MAYER-OAKES

PERSONAL: 18, 5'11", 140 lbs. Five years in racing, prior sports: lacrosse, skiing.

RACING: Best races: '73-'74 Junior World's team member; '74 National Junior Road Champion. Bikes raced: Eisentraut, Jeunet. Events: pursuit, scratch, team racing, road, time trials, stage racing "when I'm old enough." Preferred distance: long.

TRAINING: Early season miles: 200-500. Mid-season miles: "same depending on types of races." Uses intervals: "sets of four, 20/40 (hard 20 seconds, rest 40) and 30/30, only once a week well into the season. Trains 75% alone, 25% in group, 90% LSD, 5% faster than race pace, 5% intervals, some sprints. Special preparation before races: no fast riding, or intervals, no other changes. Uses weights in various combinations for legs, back, upper body. Warms up 10-20 miles fairly hard, with jumps. Important qualities: "ability to go a long way." Keeps a training diary, enters weight, miles, pulse, how he rode, other exercises. Trains by awareness of stress factors: "watch pulse in early season before fit." Winter layoff 1-2 months, x-country skiing, downhill. Winter mileage 100. Learned tactics, riding in a bunch by racing massed start road races. Never experiments with equipment changes, but sometimes alters position.

DIET: Carbo-loading unspecified. Fasts two or three times a year "to cleanse the system." During race takes "rice cakes, water, maybe sandwiches all the time as long as I'm not uncomfortably full." Uses vitamins A, D, C, B's, calcium, magnesium and E. "Only good diet is natural foods. I'm allergic to most fruits, beef, pork, potatoes, coffee and a lot of other things so my diet is rather restricted."

REASONS IN SPORT: "I look upon cycling as a career, a means toward an end and I love to ride my bike."

JOHN MEYER

PERSONAL: 23, 6'2", 170 lbs. Five years in racing, prior sports experience: one year high school track.

RACING: Best races: '74 National 10-Mile Track Championship, 7th place; '73 Indianola, Miss. race, 1st; '73 Lockport, Ill. race, 4th; '74 University of Cincinnati race, 3rd; '72 Kentucky Derby race, 4th. Bikes raced: Robbins. Events: criterium, track, road, stage races, time trials. Favorite type: criterium. Preferred distance: 20-50 miles.

TRAINING: Early season miles: 100, "increasing as it gets warmer. No hard riding until March. Start riding in January." Mid-season miles: 200. "Would like to do 250-300 but time is not available." Uses intervals: "3-5 sprints 2-3 times a week." Trains alone 5%, 95% in group, 20% LSD, 10% faster than race pace, 10% sprints, 20% medium hard distance, 20% race pace, 30% "diddling." Special preparation before races: "light workout two days before, 0-10 miles diddling one day before." No weight training. Warms up 1-10 miles medium hard before race, 3-5 easy before training. Important qualities: speed, confidence, planned aggressiveness. Keeps training diary, enters mileage only. Guidelines for training: "I try to work on my weak points." Winter layoff Nov.-Dec., will do some running this winter. Winter mileage: 0-50 Nov.-Dec., 50-100 Jan.-Feb. Learned tactics, riding in a bunch by experience, "but I feel like I can teach other riders much quicker." Experiments with equipment changes: "It doesn't have to be expensive to be good."

DIET: Uses carbo-loading 2-3 times a year, never fasts. Special pre-race diets: "I'm on a continual carbohydrate-rich diet; before a race, something which suits me at the time." During a race: "0-20 miles nothing; 30-50 miles, water; 60-120 miles, water and plenty of fruit." Never takes supplements. "No junk (candy, etc.). Just plenty of good food (lots of vegetables but some meats, fruit also). I don't like racing to interfere with what I eat and do."

REASON IN SPORT: "Personal satisfaction (ego), fitness."

JIM MONTGOMERY

PERSONAL: 30, 6'0", 170 lbs. Five years in racing, prior sports: none.

RACING: Kentucky Derby race, 1st; '73-'74 Savannah Beach, 1st; '72 Colorado State Road Championship, 2nd. Bikes raced: Cinelli, Masi, Bianchi. Events: criterium, sprints, 10-mile, 1000-meter, road, stage races. Favorite type: criterium. Preferred distance: 30-50 miles.

TRAINING: Early season miles: 200-300. Mid-season miles: 150-200. Uses intervals, type unspecified. Trains 60% alone, 40% in group, percentages unspecified except 15% sprints. Special preparation before races: one-day layoff preceded by one or more days of intervals/sprints. No weight training, warms up on rollers for 10 minutes or three miles easy. Important qualities: "good sprints, good tactics." Keeps a training diary, enters miles, pulse, weight, intervals, sprints. Training guidelines: "Train by working hard until it feels fast." Winter layoff two months. Winter mileage 100. Learned tactics, riding in a bunch by reading experience. No experiments with equipment changes.

DIET: Carbohydrate loading weekly, never fasts. Special pre-race diet: little protein, high carbohydrates. During races, takes "no food up to 50 miles, one water bottle; dried fruit, two water bottles in a race of over 50 miles." Takes vitamin C.

REASONS IN SPORT: "Satisfies my competitive urge. Fitness. Enjoy doing what I'm good at."

TIM NICHOLSON

PERSONAL: 25, 5'10", 130 lbs. Four years in racing, prior sports: seven years running (1:50.1 half-mile), college track team.

RACING: Best races: '72 Berkeley Hills, 1st; '73 Tour of Baja, 10th; '74 Tour of the Sierras, 13th; '74 Solvang, 5th; '74 Santa Cruz race, 2nd. Bikes raced: Masi, Italvega, Peter Johnson. Events: criterium, 10-mile, pursuit, road, stage races, time trials. Favorite type: stage races, criteriums. No preferred distance.

TRAINING: Early season miles: 150-200 (two-hour rides every other day with long ride on Sunday). Mid-season miles: 100-150. Uses intervals: twice a month 15 repetitions of 60 seconds on, 60 off. Trains 20% alone, 80% in group, breakdown unspecified. Special preparation before races: "Try to ride every day for two hours with layoff day before." Trains with weights in Jan. and Feb.— light, fast repetitions. Warms up "usually slow for 10 miles." Important qualities: speed and aggressiveness in last five miles of race. No training diary. Training guidelines: "usually undertrained for long distance or climbing; but try to develop good recovery rate. Winter layoff three months, running and tennis. Winter mileage: 100 and 80-mile Sunday morning ride. Learned tactics, bunch riding "mostly by experience." Does not experiment with equipment changes.

DIET: No carbo-loading, no fasting. Special pre-race diet: "get full, well-balanced meals every day." During race "prefer iced tea or Coke in water bottle for road races, water for criteriums, dates and bananas or peanut butter sandwiches to eat." No supplements.

REASONS IN SPORT: "It fulfills a number of basic human needs while exemplifying the struggle that life really is."

HANS NÜRNBERG

PERSONAL: 24, 6'1", 188 lbs. Seven years in racing, prior sports: swimming and football.

RACING: Best races: '71 National 10-mile, 1st. Bikes raced: Ron Boi. Events: criterium, mass start track, road. Favorite type: match sprint. Preferred distance: one mile.

TRAINING: Early season miles: 30-50 miles daily six or seven days a week, depending on weather. Mid-season miles: "mileage is not important here, because we're on specialized training." Does intervals, 100-150 meters 9-24 times three days a week. Trains 90% alone, 10% in group, 33% LSD, 25% intervals, 25% repetition. Special preparation before races: speed work, 15% motor sprint. Uses weights: "work the whole body doing 10 x 3 or 15 x 3 sets." Warms up "each morning beginning in April 20-30 miles." Important qualities: "since I train alone—'mental push.' " No longer keeps training diary, but used to. Training guidelines: "I'm aware of mental fatigue, so workouts are hard but short—not more than 1½ hours." Winter layoff two weeks, basketball, raquetball, weight training. Winter miles: zero. Learned tactics, riding in a bunch by riding in a pack. Sometimes experiments with equipment changes.

DIET: Carbo-loads "sometimes," doesn't fast. No special pre-race diet. During race, takes sugar tablets and water, orange or banana. Takes vitamin supplement, eats "lots of vegetables plus meats."

REASONS IN SPORT: "I enjoy the praise I receive for winning an event or race. Money from winning helps me stay in the sport but isn't the major reason for competing."

JOHN POTOTSCHNIK

PERSONAL: 29, 5'7", 160 lbs. Ten years in racing, prior sports: high school track (440).

RACING: Best races: Rockford 50-mile, 1st; Rose Bowl 94-mile, 3rd; Calif. State Road Championships, 3rd; Tour of California, 21st. Bikes raced: Jack Taylor, Masi, Fastab, Hood, Ideor ("consider Masi the best"). Events: criterium, pursuit, 10-mile, team track racing, road, stage races, time trials. Favorite type: criteriums. Preferred distance: 50 or less.

TRAINING: Early season miles: 200. Mid-season miles: 200. Does intervals "twice a week. Type varies, generally 100 rpm all-out, 150 rpm, rest, repeat." Trains "99.9% alone, .1% in group," 3% LSD, 0.5% faster than race pace, 5% intervals, 15% race pace, 1.5% long hard distance, 75% short at fast pace. Uses weights during winter, "generally medium weight and many repetitions." Warms up 5-10 miles. Important qualities: "aggressiveness, cornering ability, sprint, experience." Keeps training diary, enters date, pulse, distance, type of riding, feelings, gears, weather. Training guidelines: "Personally I depend on my pulse. If it rises five beats, for example, I take it easy." No winter layoff, does running in winter. Winter mileage: 100. Learned tactics, riding in a bunch "in a lot of races, being observant, listening to others, experience." Experiments often with equipment changes: "example, Zeus vs. Stronglight, Unica vs. Brooks."

DIET: Doesn't carbo-load, never fasts. Special pre-race diet: "I like pancakes the morning of a race—generally just eat a well-rounded diet." During a race: bananas, oranges, cookies, raisins. Drink: water, Coke, tea with honey. "Start eating after 20 miles. I don't eat or drink this every race—it varies." Takes vitamins E, B, C, A, D, eats "food as natural (organic) as possible."

REASONS IN SPORT: "To fulfill the competitive urge, for physical fitness, like to ride fast, desire to be better than average at something."

MARY JANE REOCH

PERSONAL: 28, 5'2", 120 lbs. Four years in racing, prior sports: none.

RACING: Best races: 1974 World Championships, Women's Pursuit, 4th place. Bikes raced: Masi, Eisentraut, Colnago, Limongi. Track: Colnago, Eisentraut. Events: criterium, pursuit, road, stage races, time trials. Favorite type: criterium. Preferred distance: 40-50 miles.

TRAINING: Early season miles: 100, riding four times a week. Mid-season miles: 180-250, maximum 495. Does intervals: 9 x ½-mile on, ½-mile off, and revolution intervals, twice a week. Trains 80% alone, 20% in group, 10% LSD, 15% intervals, 40% race pace, 15% jumps, sprints, 20% time trials. Special preparation before races: "I like to ride before races but shorter distance and relaxed pace—concentrate on 'feeling good.'" Trains with weights "twice a week Jan.-March, maximum weight 40 lbs., 15-minute workout." "No scheduled warmup as such." Important qualities: "Speed, spin, endurance, acceleration." Keeps training diary, enters "miles, time, aerobic points, mph, type of workout, who with." Training guidelines unspecified. Winter layoff two months, some running and x-country skiing—"try to get out on the bike strictly for fun." Winter mileage: 130. Learned tactics, riding in a bunch "by racing with men." Never experiments with equipment changes. "I have three different road bikes—but they all have the same equipment and are set up similarly."

DIET: Uses carbo-loading, but seldom, never fasts. Special pre-race diet: "high on carbohydrates if long race." During races "I eat and drink very little, nothing under 30 miles—over 30 I usually drink water and eat fruit." Takes vitamins C and E, also iron.

REASONS IN SPORT: "Racing and training heightens all of your senses—hunger, thirst, exhaustion. If you are successful there is a lot of ego reinforcement. Also, the friendships formed seem to endure because of the bond of sharing so many stresses in situations in racing."

JOE SALING

PERSONAL: 34, 6'1", 166 lbs. Nineteen years in racing, no prior sports experience.

RACING: Best races: semifinals and finals in national pursuit championships (team and individual); most satisfying victory—winning '73 Tour of Raritan for second time while wearing freshly won national jersey. Bikes raced: Paramount. Events: criterium, all track events, road, cyclo-x, time trials. Favorite type: team racing, six-day racing on board tracks. Preferred distance: 25-40 for criterium, all short time trials.

TRAINING: Early season miles: 150-200. Mid-season miles: 150-200. Does intervals "usually twice a week: 3-4 sets of approximately 2-2½ miles." Trains 100% in group, 20% LSD, 30% faster than race pace, 30% intervals, 10% sprinting. Special preparation before races: "with a race on Sunday, usually sprinting on Friday. 15-20 miles easy low gear rolling on Saturday." No weight training. Warms up 5-10 miles at approximately three-quarters race speed. Important qualities: "Aggressiveness, desire to out-perform much younger riders." Keeps training diary, enters "mileage, quality, who rode, how I felt." Training guidelines unspecified. Winter layoff month of December, x-country skiing, downhill skiing. Winter mileage: approximately 50. Learned tactics, riding in a bunch by "experience in races and training with experienced riders." Experiments with equipment changes: "I am in the bike business and try new items."

DIET: Uses carbo-loading occasionally, never fasts. Pre-race diet: "usually pancakes, coffee." During races: "short (25-30 miles) nothing unless very hot and humid; 50 miles one bottle ERG, some grapes." No supplements. "Weakness for some 'junk' foods—potato chips, ice cream, pizza, etc."

REASONS IN SPORT: "Amateur cycling is primarily an ego trip. I enjoy the compliments on a good ride—they're worth the work, time and money. Physical well-being is a great byproduct."

MICHAEL STEFFANI

PERSONAL: 30, 5'8", 155 lbs. Fifteen years in racing, prior sports: baseball.

RACING: Best races: seven state medals, approximately 100 places in first three. Bikes raced: Paramount track bike. Events: sprints and scratch races. Favorite type: mass start track races. Preferred distance: five miles.

TRAINING: Early season miles: 150-200, always on 65"-72" fixed gear. Mid-season miles: 100-150 on fixed gear of 76"-81" on road; 86"-90" on track. Does intervals: 6-10 miles moderate, 2-5 miles hard, 5-10 miles sprinting and moderate rolling. Trains 80% alone, 20% in group, 10% LSD, 60% intervals, pure sprinting on track. Special preparation before races: "No reduction except for championships, which will involve two days of gentle, short rides." Uses weights: "half-squats in off-season with as much weight as possible." Warms up "6-10 miles from easy to sprint speed in 'poco accelerando.'" Important qualities: "leg speed and explosiveness (jump)." No training diary. Training guidelines: "I either put out 100% or hang it up due to complete discouragement." No winter layoff, hiking, roller racing ('74 No. Calif. roller champion). Winter mileage: 150. Learned tactics, riding in a bunch on club rides. Experiments with equipment changes: "I use block chain for low gears and ½" roller chain for high."

DIET: Never carbo-loads, never fasts. No special pre-race diet "but I avoid greasy meat at breakfast." Before races, "at the track I'll drink about a quart of Gatorade." Takes vitamins C, E, high-potency B complex, lecithin, "Tiger's Milk" or food yeast along with normal American high-meat diet."

REASONS IN SPORT: "I train and race for enjoyment of the bicycle, and for physical and mental and spiritual well-being, and for close friendships involved with cycling; and for glory."

DALE STETINA

PERSONAL: 18, 6'0", 140 lbs. Eight years in racing, prior sports: cross-country and track.

RACING: Best races: '71 National Intermediate Road Championships, 2nd; '73 National Junior Road Championships, 3rd; '73 National Prestige Champion; won 200-mile Senior Tour of Southeast Ohio though only a junior; only junior picked for both road and track events on Junior World Championship team. Bikes raced: Ideor track bike, Paramount, Frejus, Eisentraut, Mercier, Teledyne Titan, Follis. Events: criterium, all track events, road, stage races, time trials. Favorite type: "I love them all!" Preferred distance: criterium 35-50 miles; stage race 2-4 days, 200-300 miles.

TRAINING: Early season miles: "It varies so much. I do what my body tells me to do, and I obey its warning signals. Anywhere from 160-350. LSD or fast in a *low, low* gear for agility." Mid-season miles: "160-350, only I alternate big and low gear riding, according to what my body tells me to do." Does intervals: "Usually one minute on, one minute off. From 8-10 repeats." Not done frequently. Trains less than 10% alone, more than 90% in group, 40% LSD, 10% intervals, 20% race pace, 10% long hard distance, 20% sprints. Special preparation before races: "Reduced distance enough to feel snappy on race days. Usually two days of riding under 40 miles in low gears." Not much weight training. Warms up 5-10 miles with a few wind sprints in smallest gear. Important qualities: "Aggressiveness, endurance, time-trialing ability. I use all of them often. Add hill climbing, cornering expertise, and even, upon occasion, 'wheel sucking.'" Keeps a training diary, enters distance, fatigue index, type workout, number of sprints, jams, intervals, etc. Trains by awareness of stress factors ("definitely"). Other guidelines: "ability to spin well when first mounting the bike, general feeling, pulse, length of time required to warm up, whether or not I must 'force' a warmup or whether I feel like hauling immediately. If I feel snappy and especially fresh at first, then I will ride my heart out that day. My body is ready for a workout—I hardly need a warmup. However, if I feel bad, that means 20-40 miles (not far) in my lowest three gears, warmup and down and quit." Winter layoff 2-4 months, "ride rollers every other day ½-hour, skate 1-2 hours a day, run 30 minutes every other day." Learned tactics, riding in a bunch, "racing 30 times a year for 7-8 years and from listening to Dad." Experiments with equipment changes, "and I ride light equipment."

DIET: Uses carbo-loading "for every really important race over 60 miles." Fasts once a year. Special pre-race diet: "Don't overeat for the 'energy,' but don't fast." For a race eats "only natural foods or juices (bananas, apples, grape juice, apple juice and water) solid food if longer race. Under 40 miles—water; under 20—nothing. One water bottle of juice at 40 miles." Takes "vitamins C and E every day and during races, also others." Lacto-vegetarian—"only natural foods."

REASONS IN SPORT: "Training: fitness, health, take out frustrations, go fast, get outside and to be able to race. Racing: glory, fun, ego, competitive spirit, and money (shame!)."

WAYNE STETINA

PERSONAL: 20, 5'11½", 165-170 lbs. Seven years in racing, prior sports: five years track and cross-country.

RACING: Best races: '74 World Team Trials, 1st in 14-mile time trial, 1st in 103-mile road race; '74 Tour of Newfoundland, 2nd; '73 Tour de L'Estrie, 1st; '74 World Championships, 9th place team in 100-kilometer time trial. Bikes raced unspecified. Events: criterium, pursuit, road, stage races, time trials. Favorite type: stage races. Preferred distance unspecified.

TRAINING: Early season miles: 300-400, "low gears hard." Mid-season miles: 400-500, including races—"very slow in low gears or very hard. Does intervals: 30-second interval, 10-20 repetitions, frequency unspecified. Trains 50% alone, 50% in group, 65% LSD, 10% faster than race pace, 5% intervals, 15% race pace, 5% long hard distance. Special preparation before races: "more LSD on small gears with occasional jumps and sprints (jams)." No weight training. Warms up 10-20 miles on 42 x 17-18. Important qualities: "hard training to be fit enough to race hard." No training diary. Trains by awareness of stress factors: "high pulse rate in morning or inability to warmup during training." Winter layoff, speed skating, running. Winter mileage: 0. Learned tactics, riding in a bunch in club racing and racing. Experiments with equipment changes: "light equipment, especially wheels."

DIET: Uses carbo-loading, but seldom, fasts occasionally but "not enough." Special pre-race diet: "same as training." During race: "short racing—nothing; long race—fruit juice and fruit whenever race allows." Takes vitamins E and C, calcium-magnesium combination, wheat germ. Vegetarian, eats natural foods.

REASONS IN SPORT: "Glory, bike racing is fun if you are fit enough. and win good prizes."

STAN SWAIM

PERSONAL: 38, 5'10", 180 lbs. Fifteen years in racing, prior sports: soccer, x-country skiing.

RACING: Best races: '67 Quebec-Montreal, 4th; '69 Tour of Lac St. John, 2nd; '69 Tour de la Nouvelle France, 9th. Bikes raced: Raleigh Professional. Events: road, stage races. Favorite type: stage races. Preferred distance: long.

TRAINING: Early season miles: 400-600, weather permitting. Mid-season miles: 400-600. No intervals. Trains 50% alone, 50% in group, 60% LSD, 20% race pace, 20% long hard distance. Special preparation before races: "reduced distance and an occasional layoff." No weight training: "carpentry work off-season sufficient." Warms up depending on available time. Important qualities: "endurance, determination and detachment." No training diary. Trains by awareness of stress factors: "pulse, sleep, and suppleness of legs." Winter layoff 4 months, x-country skiing when sufficient snow. Winter mileage: 0. Learned tactics, riding in a bunch: "racing (not the best way to learn!)." Does experiment with equipment changes.

DIET: Uses carbohydrate-loading once a month, never fasts. Special pre-race diet "varies every year." During race, takes "bananas, dates, ERG, tea, pears." Takes vitamins, minerals, protein supplement. "Low on meat consumption."

REASON IN SPORT: "Fitness, achievement, habit, ecological relatedness—i.e., hours and hours of wandering around old roads in Vermont."

BOB TETZLAFF

PERSONAL: 39, 5'9", 155 lbs. Twenty-five years in racing, prior sports: track, cross-country in high school.

RACING: Best races: '63 Pan-Am Games road race, team silver medal; '60

Olympic Games four-man team time trial, 11th place; '66 National Road Championships, 1st place; second place in two stages of Canadian tour against Russian riders. Bikes raced: Cinelli, Paramount, Rickert, Follis, Allegro, Peugeot, etc. Events: criterium, all track events, road, cyclo-x, stage races, time trials. Favorite type: road. Preferred distance: 60-90 miles

TRAINING: Early season miles: 200-400. Mid-season miles—350-500. Uses intervals, type and frequency vary. "Sometimes sprints, sometimes jumps, sometimes 30 seconds on, 30 seconds off." Trains 70% alone, 30% group, 30% LSD, 5% faster than race pace, 5% intervals, 10% race pace, 10% long hard distance. Special preparation before races: "Layoff one or two days or reduced distance and easy riding (5-10 miles). Weight training: Exergenie—leg push and pull. Warms up 15-20 minutes at 15 mph. Important qualities: "aggressiveness, endurance, 'psych,' sprinting." Keeps training diary "sometimes," enters miles, type of ride, sprints. Trains by awareness of stress symptoms: "When overwork or allergy bother me, I cut down and go easy." Winter layoff 2-3 months, running, volleyball, exercises. Winter mileage: 50-100. Learned tactics, riding in a bunch "by long years of experience, and from an old Italian coach." Does not experiment with equipment change.

DIET: Uses carbo-loading, frequency unspecified, fasts occasionally. Special pre-race diet: pancakes. During races, "Every 20 minutes small bread items like fig newtons, bananas, other fruits. Drink water or coffee. Takes vitamins A, B, C, D, E, calcium, magnesium, minerals. Eats natural foods, "but not fanatic."

REASONS IN SPORT: "glory, fitness, fun."

DONNA TOBIAS

PERSONAL: 30, 5'2", 115 lbs. Twelve years in racing, no prior sports.

RACING: Best races: '69 National Road Race Championships, 1st. '70 White Mountain Hundred, 15th; '68 Far West Track Championship, 1st on points; '74 10-mile time trial, 3rd in 24:29; Bikes raced: Cinelli, CID ("the Cinelli handles better"), Brian Rourke. Events: pursuit, sprint, handicap, criterium, road, stage races, time trials, no favorites or preferred distances.

TRAINING: Early season miles: "as much as my admittedly inadequate sleep will allow. Mid-season miles: 200. Does intervals: 30 on and 30 off; also, 200-350 strokes followed by long rest. Solo and group training percentages vary, type unspecified. Takes one day's rest before a race. Uses weights only in winter, on a Universal gym for leg exercise. Warms up 45 minutes on a low gear. Important qualities: "I have been successful only when I was aggressive." Keeps a training diary, enters miles, energy level, type of training. Trains by awareness of stress factors—unusually high pulse upon waking. Winter layoff dictated by weather, rides rollers. Learned tactics, riding in a bunch "I never did." Never experiments with equipment changes.

DIET: Occasionally uses carbo-loading, never fasts. No pre-race diet. During races takes "water to drink, bananas for food." No supplements.

REASONS IN SPORT: "I feel better when I'm in training than when I'm not."

5

Putting
It All Together

Roger St. Pierre is a well-known cycle racing journalist, photographer and author from England. He has raced successfully himself, and recently served as Team Manager for British juniors riding the Tour of Newfoundland and a series of Canadian and American one-day classics. Roger's book "Cycle Racing Tactics" is recommended for anyone who wants a detailed treatment of the subject.

It is often argued that road racing is something of a lottery—that the best man doesn't always win. I would disagree, since sheer physical ability isn't the only factor that should be considered in evaluating a victory. Bike handling, tactical sense, ability to suffer and sheer luck all play a part and rightly so. The best rider almost always does win because he is the one who has turned all these factors, luck included, to his advantage.

So how does one narrow all the odds and improve one's chances, given that physical strength and fitness have already been assured?

First and foremost, make a careful study of the particular race's planned route and if possible take a training ride over it. Are the roads hilly or flat? exposed or sheltered; winding or straight; narrow or broad; well or badly surfaced? It's amazing how many riders will start in a race without even knowing how many laps there are or where the finish is located. Bear in mind though, that a course will take on a different aspect when racing in a bunch than it does when reconnoitered at training speeds. Corners that looked easy may become frighteningly dangerous at higher speeds, Conversely, many hills will seem flattened when you are at racing speeds on hitting the bottom and starting to swoop upwards.

Know your opponents, too. Study their form and learn their preferred tactics. Are they climbers or sprinters? Where do they usually attack? If you don't know the dangermen by sight, then write their numbers on your forearm with a ballpen so that you can mark their attacks. In place-to-place events it also helps to write a list of place names on your arm together with the distance from each to the finish.

Gamesmanship plays a big part in the bike game and I remember riding a race back in the '60s when a blisteringly hot day and a shelterless undulating course of 90 miles spelled sheer purgatory.

I made sure that I carried two feeding bottles of water, a damp sponge in my rear pocket and another tucked down the back of my jersey to protect my neck from the sun. Drinking too much in such conditions leads to a disastrous craving, so my water was not for consumption but for use as a cooling spray.

Of course, it wasn't long before other riders started trying to cadge a drink from me but each time I refused and put the bottle to my own lips. As we passed the changing rooms each lap more riders retired, tempted by the waters of a village pump, gushing tantalizingly at the roadside. Eventually just six of us were left out of 40 starters and after our sprint finish one of these survivors came up to me and said: "Well, now you can give me a drink, can't you?"

I just smiled and answered: "No, both my bottles have been empty for the last 30 miles!"—and they had been! Indeed, I'd been as thirsty as anyone but by pretending to drink I'd demoralized my rivals and kept my own spirits up. Equally devastating is the ploy of tipping the remaining contents of a bottle into the road after you've drunk your fill.

If you take plenty of food and drink you'll often find you don't need it and can get through the race on very little. On the other hand, if you don't take enough it's easy to start mentally craving for more.

Remember, don't let the excitement of a race make you forget to eat. Once hunger knock comes it's too late to do anything about it, even if you've got food with you. Little and often should be your guiding rule.

Perhaps it's best to explain tactics by looking at how one man in particular goes about it. Let's call our fictional character Jim. He's not a star rider, just a man of average ability, but one who uses his brains as well as his legs.

As they line up, Jim is to be found in the front ranks for he knows that even in an 80-miler like today's outing the vital break can go from the start. Sure enough, as the flag drops one of the favorites charges off the front with two others in tow. Sensing the danger, Jim closes the gap wtih one flat-out effort before it gets too big (it's easier to get across a gap quickly with a sprint-type effort than to try to reduce it steadily).

Knowing that he hasn't the strength to last the whole race in such a small breakaway group, Jim doesn't want it to succeed so he makes sure he takes other riders up to it with him. Catching the leaders, he takes a short breather than goes to the front as though doing his turn; but instead of maintaining the pace he eases slightly and each time his turn at the front comes round he does the same thing, his soft-pedalling marring the group's efficiency and enabling the bunch to re-catch them.

As the junction is made everyone eases, but well aware that this is just the moment when another break could be successfully launched, Jim stays near the front, watching for any such moves. However, everything settles down and the bunch plugs along the fairly flat roads into a nagging headwind.

Jim is now sitting about eight places from the front, getting plenty of shelter but well placed to mark any attacks. Though he keeps close to the wheel in front, he rides slightly to one side, in case the man in front should get out of the saddle and kick back, and giving himself room for evasive action should anyone switch or fall in front. Already he has noted the men whose bike-handling isn't too hot and keeps clear of them, lessening the risk of a crash.

Jim doesn't just watch the wheel in front, he's aware of what's happening at the front of the bunch, ever alert for attacks or pileups, his hands resting on the tops of the brake levers, giving him a comfortable position but keeping his brakes in easy reach. Jim only uses those brakes sparingly and avoids snatching at them or swerving violently, endangering those behind.

After 10 miles or so, Jim senses that his front tire is softening so he seeks out his teammates and lets them know. Luckily they have a following car so he'll get a wheel change. Up goes an arm, both to warn fellow competitors that he is about to stop and to let his team car know he needs help. As he slips out of the bunch he points to his front wheel.

The team car passes Jim and stops 30 yards up the road, so that before he even comes to a halt the mechanic is waiting at the roadside with a wheel at the ready. Jim snicks into low gear ready for a quick re-start and on stopping places both feet on the ground. Instead of dismounting, he lifts the front wheel off the ground so that the mechanic can remove it and slip in the new one. The mechanic pushes him back into action and Jim gets his head down, knowing he's got to get back onto the bunch quickly. It's no good trying to time trial back—you'll never make it—so he sprints all-out in an effort to get back within a mile or so.

Our man has three teammates in the race. One goes to the front and does his best to slow things down by messing up the changes and going through slowly, one drops off the bunch and waits for Jim, and the third sits right on the tail of the bunch.

When Jim gets up to his teammate they start pace-sharing, with short, fast stints at the front, working their way through the following vehicles until they are about 50 yards from the tail of the bunch, at which point the third teamman drops back for them and paces them the final effort onto the bunch.

Once safely in contact, they don't linger at the back but make their way to the middle where they will get an easier ride, be able to watch out for any attacks, and miss the whiplash effect which always makes things hard for those who sit on the back. It's a simple fact that, except on a dead-straight road into a headwind, the back is far from being the easiest spot in a bunch.

Riders who are hanging on, or about to be dropped get in the way, letting gaps open; there's more likelihood of becoming involved in crashes, either as a direct victim or by being caught behind those who have fallen; and, most importantly, there's that whiplash effect—as you are slowing down to go into a corner, the front riders are already sprinting out of it, creating an "accordion" effect which strings out the bunch and gives the hardest ride to those at the back.

Jim keeps in a moderately low gear, pedalling comfortably, recovering from his effort. Now the race is on a twisting section with a succession of corners. Jim takes these the correct way—not hurtling into them at breakneck speed, braking (and thus losing control) in the turn and then having to accelerate away again from a very low speed. No, Jim enters the corner at a modest pace then accelerates through it so that he already has a fair speed going as he comes out. Braking while actually in a corner is—as with an automobile—the quick way to skids, loss of control and a nasty crash. Moreover, it's the angle of lean, rather than actually turning the handlebars, which carries a bike through a corner at speed. The expert keeps his knees tucked in—there's more control that way—and heels the bike over gently, letting it find the right line rather than fighting it.

Jim enters the corners wide then cuts across the apex, thus minimizing the angle of turn and, by retaining most of his speed with these correct techniques, minimizes the need to get out of the saddle and risk wheelspin on damp roads.

Attacking out of a corner is an oft-employed tactic, but it's often more effective to jump away to a small lead just before a corner then increase it through the curve by taking the right line—which those in a bunch cannot always do.

One of the least-well-understood but most vital of road racing techniques is that of echelon riding—in other words, obtaining the maximum possible shelter from adverse winds. If the wind is coming from the right, then sit to the left of the rider in front. In a total cross-wind situation, the correct position will be almost alongside the leading rider, on his leeward side.

What goes wrong, though, is that when the road changes direction riders neglect to change the side on which they swing off after doing their turn of pacemaking at the front. When the wind is from the right, the leading rider should be sitting in the right hand gutter so that the other riders can fan out to his left. After his turn, he should drop back down the line, taking shelter from each rider in turn till he reaches the tail of the echelon. When the wind direction changes, the procedure should change with it—that is, the lead rider sitting in the center of the road with the rest fanned out to his right.

Soon the first hill looms up and, being a poor climber, Jim places himself towards the front of the bunch so that he can climb at his own pace, gradually slipping back through the group but still being in contact over the top. What's more, climbing at the back of a bunch from the start means that other struggling riders will tend to balk you. Another worthwhile emthod is to single out a known strong but smooth-riding climber and sit glued to his wheel, concentrating one's eyes on his whirring gears or pumping legs and inducing an almost hypnotic effect which will help carry you over the hill you fear. But don't break that concentration before the top, as one glance upwards at the still seemingly far-off summit can be devastating to your morale.

Uphill is another favorite place for attacks to be launched but often more effective is the gambit of launching an attack just after the summit has been reached, at that moment when everyone is relaxing after the effort. Jim makes sure he's near the front as the descent starts in earnest, for not only can be watch for such attacks but he will also be able to descend safely, picking his own line through corners without being obstructed by others.

The art of smooth, fast, safe descending is to think ahead. Don't just concentrate on the corner you are tackling, but make sure you are lining up right for the next one. Sit well back, thus keeping the back wheel firm on the road. Use brakes sparingly and with out snatching at them; squeeze, don't jerk.

Moving nearer to the front, Jim slipstreams each rider in turn, pulling round at the last moment, passing closely, then slipping in behind the next man ahead, thus moving up the line with a minimum of effort.

Too many people seem to believe you have to have tough hills to make a race hard but some of the most demanding conditions come on flat roads with a fierce tailwind—as anyone who has raced in Holland will tell you. In these conditions nobody gets much shelter and the pace is hellish—and once again, those near the front get it easier than the tail-enders. Gaps will keep opening near the back and these have to be filled quickly before they become too large and impossible to close.

Despite the speed, a break has gone now, the snaking peloton of riders having split into several groups, the leading foursome moving slowly ahead. Jim has a teammate up there but he's working hard at the front of the chasers. Why? Because he knows his teammate has no sprint and anyway is unlikely to last the distance. If the break stays clear the team's chances will vanish; better then to pull this teammate and his breakaway companions back; after all he might be able to get away in a more favorable group later on.

Jim's teammate knows the situation too, and is sitting on the back of the leading group getting an easy ride so that should they stay clear, he will at least have a better chance than normal at the finish.

Jim has the chasers organized into a working echelon, each man doing a short, sharp 50-yard or so stint at the front, then dropping back down the line, not all at once but slowly, so that as the next rider swings off the front he sits on his wheel until the back is reached and he starts moving up the line again. With a final effort the gap is closed and the two groups join up; but instead of the usual lull in pace—one of the best moments to launch a counter-attack—this time the speed stays up and Jim begins suffering. He doesn't let the others know it, though; he continues to work in the line but goes through a bit more slowly and does shorter turns at the front, until he feels even weaker and begins to miss his turns—every second or third one at first until eventually he is not working at all.

On a short, sharp drag he is actually dropped, losing 50 yards or so, but rather than trying to save energy he makes an all-out effort over the top, sprinting to get back on for he knows it is fatal to hang just off the back as this saps morale as well as physical strength. If you are dropped, for any reason the maxim must always be—get back on the group as quick as you can, with an all-out, do-or-die effort. Better to take the chance of blowing up completely than to conserve strength in order to finish off the back.

As there are tactics for victims, there are tactics for torturers too, and sensing Jim's weakness one of the stronger riders decides to try to get rid of him for good. As Jim rejoins, this man is at the back and lets a gap open, so that Jim has to go round him to close it. Repeated several times, this tactic usually works, but it depends on the "executioner" being strong and confident enough to close the gap himself once the victim is dispatched. Luckily for Jim, this rival isn't strong enough himself to try it more than a couple of times.

Breakaway groups often form almost by accident when someone lets a gap open—before they know it the leaders have a working advantage. But more often it's a case of riders sprinting off the front in ones and twos and then joining up to make a working group "up the road." There are lots of breaks in this race and each time they are brought back the bunch eases as riders get second wind, taking a needed drink or some food. It is this off-guard situation which makes such times ideal for counter-attacks.

Jim's feeling better now and he goes with one of these attacks, since it contains several of the favorites. At first they set a ferocious pace but once a 'working lead has been established they settle down to a steady, efficient routine, each man doing his fair share of pace-making.

Now Jim is completely over his earlier rough patch and in fact seems strongest of all. But he doesn't tear them apart. He knows it's still a long way to the finish and he needs their help to get there without being caught by the frantically chasing bunch, biding his time till the moment arrives when he will be near enought to the finish to make a lone effort.

He picks his moment perfectly. As the others have eased to take drinks and food, riding along on the tops, he jumps from the back of the group, pass-ing the leader as closely as possible giving a demoralizing impression of greater speed, then switching to the other side of the road so nobody can get onto his wheel. His first effort is virtually flat-out sprinting, but once clear he settles down to a steady effort knowing this is less strength-sapping than uneven bursts of speed.

Placing himself well on the road he takes full advantage of the wind shelter offered by roadside hedges and walls, keeping close to the curb, out of the wind. He has a teammate in the group behind and that man is doing a fine job of ob-structing the chase. Each time someone sets off in pursuit he is on their wheel, then when they swing off to let somebody else take a spell at the front he ambles through, breaking the rhythm. When in the middle of the group, he lets gaps open, breaking up the fluidity of their efforts. In turn they try to squeeze him out of the line and keep him to the back where he will be unable to obstruct.

Soon Jim has a healthy two minutes in hand, but as the finish draws ever nearer this lead starts to tumble. He doesn't panic into a rash effort which will only see him blow up, but paces himself well, hoping his lead will be enough. It isn't, and two miles from home he is re-caught, What's more, the bunch in turn catches the breakaways and it is all on for the sprint.

Jim still has a chance. He has studied the finish and noted that the road dips till 200 yards to go, then rises slightly to the line, so he keeps his gear reasonably low, knowing it is easier to change up than down while sprinting—and more acceptable to tired legs, too.

The wind is coming from the left now, so Jim makes sure he is inside a wheel and getting some shelter as the sprint begins—and he's made sure to choose the wheel of a strong sprinter who can be relied on to stick at the front and give a good lead out.

While he's inside that wheel, Jim takes care to make sure he doesn't get boxed in, knowing that with everyone trying to get shelter the right-hand side of the bunch will get congested.

Jim's teammate is tucked in just behind him and with 100 yards to go Jim jumps past the two leaders. As he does so his teammate slows slightly, thus balking Jim's two closest rivals who had been tucked in behind. With 50 yards to go Jim hits the front. A rival desperately bids to get inside his wheel but Jim switches to the outside so this challenger can get no shelter.

Victory is Jim's but he doesn't put his arm up in a victory salute until he is sure his wheel is over the line—too many races have been lost in that manner, to the great embarrassment of the over-confident riders concerned. Remember, never ease until you've actually corssed the line; there's always a chance of someone getting past with a late effort.

I could go on beyond this account of just one fictional but based-on-reality race and write a whole book on road racing tactics, but there's only space here to add a few more general hints—a sort of "Ten Commandments" or raicng—though far more than 10 in number:

● Use your energies effectively. If you get in a break and it doesn't seem to have any chance of staying clear, then don't bust a gut in useless endeavor—sit in till it is caught and save your energies for a break which does have real chances.

● When delayed by punctures, crashes or other reasons, rejoin the bunch as rapidly as possible and don't wait for teammates unless they have a real chance of regaining the field with your help—better for a team to lose one man than two.

● Don't give other riders an armchair ride. If you are in a break with someone who will not work, get rid of him by letting gaps open then jumping across them. If he's too wcak to work then he's a hindrance and could still prove a danger in the finish—it's amazing what the sight of the checkered flag can do to a seemingly shattered rider's adrenalin.

If you can't ditch such a non-worker then he's probably a sprinter saving himself for the gallop, in which case get the others in the break to help give him a hard ride by taking him off the back in turns so that he has to keep closing gaps—he'll soon decide it is easier to do his share of work at the front.

● If there's a break and none of your team is in it, then do your share to pull it back—there's no point sitting in while victory slips away up the road.

● Team tactics should make sense—there's no point in blocking a chase just to protect a single teammate in a break of 10. What if he punctures, crashes or is dropped?—all your chances will have goine.

● Really effective teamwork should be aggressive, not defensive. The real classic is to get one or two of your men away, then send up reinforcements to join them one at a time. This is done by placing all your riders at the head of the field. One will jump clear, the others will ease to allow a gap to open, then the tactic is repeated for each of the other team-men until—ideally—the whole team is clear. The idea is to get as many of your men away as possible with as few of the opposition as is possible. If you manage to get two or three away with a couple of rivals then you are doing well.

Of course, the trouble with such a move is that if there are too many riders from one team in a break then the rivals may decide not to work with it. This happened to the Great Britain team I was managing in the 1974 Tour of Newfoundland. We had three men away with one Quebec rider, one US rider and two Ontario team-men. It was the last stage and if the group stayed clear, we could not only jump up the individual standings of this stage race but also win the overall team prize. Naturally, the American wasn't working as the US were team leaders, nor was the Quebec man as team were lying second. The Ontario men were not too keen either, because they felt our three would have no trouble working them over in the sprint.

Our obvious tactic then was to give the Ontario men an incentive to help our men stay clear so I called one of our riders back to the team car and gave him instructions to tell the Ontario riders that if they helped the break stay clear our boys would help them win the stage. This gambit worked in that we immedi-

ately had two willing helpers, but as it happened another American got up to
the group with two others so we still didn't win the team award though we jump-
ed to second place.

• Psychology plays a great part in the bike game—a bit of whistling or
singing while climbing a tough hill can have a devastating effect on your rivals'
morale. Don't let the others know when you are suffering. If someone is constantly attacking, going through fast, tell him to get a move on—it'll shatter his
confidence if he thinks you are finding it easy just when he's trying to make it
hard. Always remember—when it's hurting you, it's hurting everyone else, too.

• When launching an attack, choose the moments when your rivals are
off guard—drinking or eating, relaxing after a climb or easing for a corner.

• If there is a crash or a puncture, be ready for the almost certain acceleration as others in the bunch take advantage of the victims' misfortunes.

• When riding criterium races on small, tight circuits, it is especially important to stick near the front. Try to overlap someone else as you go through
a corner. Then as they get out of the saddle and sprint down the next straight
you can easily slip into their slipstream without having to make a big effort. A
bunch will always string out after a corner, but if you are at the front going into
it then you can afford to drop back through the bunch out of the corner, conserving strength before moving up easily to the front as the bunch begins to slow
for the next turn.

• Inexperienced riders use their brakes far too much and this is the prime
cause of crashes. Going into a corner, don't sit right on a wheel but to one side
of it in case the rider suddenly hits his brakes causing a touching of tires and a
possible spill.

• It is in the field of stage racing—events spread over several days—that
team tactics really become important. If you have no accepted team leader then
the best bet is to ride the first stage as a normal road race, see who is riding
best, then start working on his behalf from stage two onwards—but never put all
your hopes on just one man. Any rider who loses a lot of time will be required
to forget his own chances—which have gone anyway—and become a workhorse
for the better-placed men, limiting his own ambitions to a possible stage win.

Fatigue has an accumulative effect in stage racing so beware going for long
breakaways in the early stages.

Try to get your best placed man in all the vital moves—along with others
of the team to aid him should he have trouble. If your top men miss a break and
it contains their most dangerous rivals don't work with it but sit in and try to
hinder the efficient progress of its efforts. Then there is every chance of it being
re-caught, but should it still stay clear then you will at least have a maximum
chance of taking the stage win for your team.

However tired or far behind you are, do not retire unless you are physically too exhausted to continue. Your own overall chances may be gone but you
can still help your teammates and maybe get a stage win later on.

Don't try for too much. To many teams have lost everything by trying to
take all the prizes—individual, team, king of the mountains and so on—then
running out of steam.

Don't just look after one man; have a reserve leader and try to keep him well placed too—in case the top man runs out of steam.

● Given another 100 pages I could fill them all and still not have told everything there is to know about road racing tactics. Even Eddy Merckx learns something new every day—but that is after all one of the attractions of our fascinating sport. At least, I hope I've given enough insight of the basics to enable you to learn the rest from your own experience and observations.

TRACK EVENTS

Cycle track racing is not only one of the most thrilling of all sports—both from the competitor and spectator angles—but encompasses a wide diversity of specialized events, from the split second explosive action of the two-up sprint to the finesse of the miss-and-out, from the smooth action of the pursuit to the noise of the motor pace. However, despite a wide range of events, the really good trackman can adapt to all of them—though he is bound to be better at some than at others. Thus Patrick Sercu is not only the current king of the six-day circus but also one of the fastest match-race sprinters the world has ever seen.

MATCH SPRINT RACES
The most coveted of all track titles has always been the sprint, mainly because it is not only a straight forward clash between two men (at least, in the finals) but because it employs the mind as well as muscle. From the front, from the back, with a long effort or a short one, the sprint can be won in many ways, but the essence of classic sprinting is in beating your rival by outwitting him. Few riders have the sheer strength to simply sit on the front and roar a following rider off their wheel. The sheer mechanics of cycling mean that the man behind has to make far less effort because the wind barrier is being broken for him by the lead rider. So it is obvious that if you lead out all the way, with a man glued to your wheel, he should—all other things being equal—have no trouble coming round you down the finishing straight and winning.

There are times when a rider's best, maybe only, chance lies in going for a long, all-out effort, but it will only work if he can open a big gap at the start, leaving the other man fighting hard to close up on him. This can be done either with a good push and an explosive jump right from the start, or he must lay back slightly then take a dive off the banking; but either method will only work if the rival is caught off guard. Usually, though, the opening section of any sprint is pure maneuvering, the real effort only coming in the final 250-300 meters. Up till then the riders will have been jockeying for position.

Some sprinters have an almost pathological fear of leading out—leading to those stand-still demonstrations as they try to force their rival into the lead, but the really clever rider will not necessarily find the front-running position any

disadvantage. The big fear of leading, of course, is that the following rider will pull a fast one, jumping away to an unbeatable lead while you are unsighted.

But why be unsighted? On a sunny day, shadows can show you exactly what the man behind is up to and, in any case, if you know the track well, you should be able to ride around it looking back over your shoulder the whole way and knowing, from how much straight is behind you, just where the next turn commences. If you should need to glance ahead to reassure yourself that you aren't running into the fence, then simply keep your head turned half-way, so that with a quick sideways glance you can see where you are going without your rival being aware your eyes are no longer on him.

Sooner or later your rival will have to make a break for the line and by leading out you will be at an advantage. For a start, you are at least a length and a half in front of him when he starts his effort, which gives you the chance of matching him when he makes his effort—even if he has a much faster jump. As he makes his effort down the inside you can shut down on him, taking him down to the inside gutter, in which case he will have to ease and then go round the outside, giving you the chance to jump into a winning lead.

If your man has a renowned jump, then lead out fairly fast so as to blunt the edge of his initial spurt. If you are leading out and want to make your own big effort from the front, then box your opponent against the rails and keep him pinned inside your back wheel until you are ready to make a dive for the line. Since he doesn't know when this is going to come, you should be able to snatch at least a two-length lead even though he has you sighted. Should he ease off to get out of the box then you can either ease back with him, to keep him in it, or use that moment to make your big effort. If you want him to lead out the final effort, then you can let him slip by inside you and latch onto his wheel without having to make quite as voilent an acceleration as he had done.

Should you choose to ride the race from the back, letting the other rider lead away from the start, your object will be to catch him off guard, unless you know that you have a totally superior finish—in which case you can simply stick to his wheel, follow him wherever he goes, getting an armchair ride until you choose to go round him and cruise past.

Riding from the back, make your man worry what you are up to. If he keeps looking round then glancing forward again, time your jump for the precise moment when he has just looked back and is beginning to turn forward. That way he will be unsighted until you are already past him and on your way to victory.

Get to know your opponents and their favorite ways of winning and then work out tactics to draw their sting. It's amazing how often a clever sprinter can beat a much faster man. Gamesmanship plays an important role. Sailing close to the rules but not breaking them, you can keep a man pinned down to the inside of the track so that he has to slow and then go round the outside, or you can ride an overtaking rider wide so that he has to drop back and then go for the inside when you can close him into a box.

HANDICAP RACES
Handicap racing calls for quite different techniques. Here it's a case of

getting off the mark as quickly as possible, so make sure your pusher is a strong, burly fellow with lots of arm-power.

Start with your cranks absolutely vertical and with your right leg at the top so that you will drive into the banking as you start, rather than going into a wobble. Your pusher's effort will carry the cranks over the top-dead-center, leaving you with a full half-revolution starting effort from your lead leg.

Try to relax. If your legs are tense at the start then they will work against the pusher's throw. The pusher should be in stockinged feet, rather than wearing shoes, as he'll get more grip from the track that way.

Go on the whistle rather than the gun, as by the time the brain has registered the message and passed it to the legs the gun will be firing anyway so you will not have cheated. Rise out of the saddle but don't put your weight too far over the front wheel as this will cause wasted effort through back wheel spin.

However long the race, make an all-out starting effort so that you can get up with the longmarkers as quickly as possible; you can then tuck in behind them getting shelter or go straight past depending on how much of the race remains. If you start off the front mark, still go all-out—it's often possible to lead from start to finish. But should the others latch onto your wheel, do not tow them round but let them past; then latch in behind them and make an effort at the finish to get round them again.

MASSED START RACES

Bunched distance races call for similar tactics to road racing—and that includes riding off to one side of a lead rider to gain shelter in a cross-wind. Many tracks have freak wind conditions, so get to know just which way the wind will be coming from on each section of the track and ride accordingly, getting as much shelter as possible from the other riders.

Be alert for splits in the bunch and fill them straightaway rather than waiting till they become serious and a big effort is called for.

Bunch racing is often erratic, and with only one fixed gear, this can be hell on the legs. Remember, when going for primes or finishing sprints you cannot change up a gear, so you'll need to be nearer the front than is often the case at the start of a sprint on the road.

Try to pick a good rider's wheel and follow it. Look for a man who is strong but has a smooth pedalling action. That way you are neither likely to miss out on the breaks nor have your legs torn off by stop-start riding efforts.

Use the bankings to advantage. If the bunch has slowed and you want to try for a breakaway, swing up to the top, then make a dive past the leaders, using the downgrade of the banking for your initial acceleration.

A good time to attack is often with a couple of laps to go when the sprinters are all juggling for position and watching each other. Should you stick for a sprint then get on a good fast wheel and stick near the front, about third or fourth down the line. If you are strong but not too fast then it is best to lead out. If you've got a good jump then come off a wheel.

MISS–AND–OUT

Miss-and-out races in many ways call for more mental than physical resources, for it is clever maneuvering and lightning reactions which usually win such events. They can be won from the front or from the back, but the former is the safer method. For a start, you get a much smoother ride, the accelerations at the front as you race for the line each lap being mild compared with those at the back where not only do you need more speed but you are also in danger of being balked. It's best to sit third or fourth in the line for the whole race.

Remember, it is the last *back wheel* across the line which decides who is eliminated. If you ease as your front wheel hits the line there is always the chance that the man who is half a wheel behind will come past fast enough to get his back wheel home first and that means you, not he, will be out.

Pick the gaps to go through and once you've made a decision stick with it—there's no time for changes of mind. If the gaps start closing then just plow through. If you are riding a straight line there's no reason why you should fall or bring your rivals down, even though you end up touching shoulders on each side!

It's usually best to go round the outside, too—if only because the judges, being on the infield, are more likely to call out the number nearest to them should it be a close one. If you are on the outside their line of vision is likely to be obscured and as theirs is a split-second, almost impulsive decision, you could well get away with it.

If two riders are being called out each lap, then never try to ride from the back as it is too easy to come unstuck, especially as things can get confused by riders eliminated earlier failing to leave the field and making you think you are safe when you aren't.

Don't ever drop out incidentally, unless you are absolutely sure it is your number the judges have called—never take the other riders' word for it. If it was you then the judges will make very sure you hear your number next time round!

If only one rider is to be called out each lap you can ride from the back, picking off rivals one by one by making sure that as you come round each time you have one man pinned inside your back wheel while you stay close enough to the infield to prevent him slipping through. All he can do is ease back to get out of the box and go round the outside but if you ease with him he is still in the box and certain of elimination. Always be careful, though, of groups sneaking off the front as you will be out of the running entirely should you miss such a winning move—your aid at the back being whittled down each lap as riders are eliminated.

Once in the final two or three laps, of course, the race becomes more of a straightforward trial of speed and strength—but up till then the clever rider can outlast many faster but less astute men.

POINTS RACES

Points and course-des-primes races are often very erratic events. Plan the laps you are going to go for. It's better to win one lap of a course-des-primes and get a prize for your efforts than come second in five laps and win nothing.

Keep to the front all the time, just following the sprinters' wheels on those laps where you aren't actually trying to win the sprint. These races usually split up and if you fail to get into the front group you're in a race to nowhere.

Go for laps you really feel you can win, in other words those when the opposition looks weakest (for instance, when the real fast men are recovering from a big effort the previous lap).

UNKNOWN DISTANCE

In an unknown distance race always stay in the first half dozen, as there will, be little time to move up once the bell for the final lap is rung—and you never know exactly when that is going to be.

1000-M TIME TRIAL

Kilometer time trials are a very specialized event calling for a lot of self-knowledge; but the real art is to get as fast a start as possible then try to hang on to the finish rather than start slow then build up speed. Again, go on the whistle, not the gun.

PURSUITING

Individual pursuiting is an extended form of the kilometer, except that you have a rival on the other side of the track, and it is perhaps the purest and toughest form of track racing.

Again, ride to your own capabilities and don't be panicked by the opposition. If the man is a super-fast starter don't try to hold him and blow up—let him take a lead then whittle it down, which is sure to demoralize him.

On a very small track, beware the man who will put everything into an all-out effort to actually catch you, knowing that if he does so he will not have to cover the full distance—that's a tactic Ferdi Bracke used in taking Hugh Porter's world title from him in Antwerp some years back.

Once your rival gets into the same straight as you the game is almost inevitably up because he'll have such a great psychological boost plus a measure of slipstreaming to enable him to catch you.

Have a helper at the trackside to let you know how you stand—thumbs up when you are leading, thumbs down when you are behind—and letting you know how many laps remain, so that you can put all your concentration into your own riding, concentration being the secret of successful pursuiting.

Don't let your muscles stiffen between rounds—use a pair of rollers or ride round the infield on a low-geared road bike, and use a silk jersey for your riding rather than a woolen one as this creates less wind drag.

Team pursuiting success depends on picking men who may not be the best individually but who are evenly matched together. Never start your weakest man immediately in front of the strongest man as he'll do his turn, swing off and never get back on again as the strong man steps up the pace. Nor should he start immediately behind the strongest man, either, as he'll have to fight so hard to hold that man's front-running effort that he'll have nothing left for his won turn. Use one of your middle men as first starter, rather than the fastest man, as the latter is liable to lear the team apart before it has a chance to settle into a rhythm.

Half-lap changes are best on a big track but if one rider is clearly strongest then he can do full laps. Smooth, efficient changes are vital. Riders who swing up early leaving the next man to do a longer turn are deadly, especially if that following rider is going through a weak patch—the thought of that extra distance up front can totally demoralize him.

The technique is to wait till you get to the end of the straight, then instead of following the turn carry straight on up the banking; then, as the others slip through inside sweep down to click onto the back of the line—without leaving a gap for yourself to close.

When your turn at the front comes don't sprint through, as this will make it difficult for the relieved rider to latch onto the back. Go through steadily and make a gradual acceleration to peak effort just before it is your turn to swing off.

MADISON RACING

Madison races are thrilling, often confusing affairs. On the small indoor six-day tracks, laps are constantly being won and lost but lap gains are very infrequent on the big outdoor tracks, most races being decided on points. Since most American amateur racing is under such conditions, it is apparent that each team needs a good sprinter plus a strong workhorse if it is to be a winning pair.

Tactically, madisons are similar to all bunch races, the one big difference coming in that all important section—the changes. When coming in for a change start rolling from the top of the banking when your partner is still 75 yards or so behind, get into the saddle quickly and run down to the inside of the track so that your partner will pass just inside you at about 2-3 mph faster speed. Don't move so fast he has to struggle to catch you, or come down so late he misses you!

If you haven't proper madison shorts with a built-in pad, put a home-made softly-padded roll about 6" long and 1½" diameter down your shorts on the left-hand buttock side. Your partner can then grip this to give you an efficient throw.

Take care that other riders do not balk you when they change in front. Go over the top so that you can slip straight onto the wheel of the rider being thrown in, rather than being caught behind the rider who is coming out.

When your turn to be relieved arrives, stay on the drops till the last possible moment, then when 10 yards or so behind your partner, switch your left hand to the tops of the bars, right in against the stem and raise your right hand, grabbing your partner's madison pad, and throw him in. Never attempt to ride on the drops while throwing as this will cause you to wobble dangerously.

If you are dropped by the string, make a big effort to get back in contact within a couple of laps. If you fail to do so, don't stay in limbo half-a-lap in arrears but concede the lap, for while it means you have to pull a full lap back later on if you want to go for overall victory, it at least means you are back in the running for the sprint awards. If you were to stick half-a-lap in arrears you would simply be racing for nothing at all.

Losing a lap needn't be disastrous, and losing it rapidly means you will not be wasting energy needlessly which could be put to better use later on in either picking up sprint points or in trying to regain that lap when the rival teams have weakened somewhat. There are other track

There are other track specialties too—notably motor-paced racing—but these are rarely seen in the US. The above advice only glosses the surface of what is a complex and highly technical sport but hopefully it will help you avoid the more obvious mistakes which many riders are still making after years of experience simply because nobody has ever pointed them out.

Hopefully, one day there will be enough experienced, fully qualified coaches around so that everyone can be given practical tuition—which, after all, is the best, maybe the only, real way to learn.

6
Racing's Country Counsin

Tom Cuthbertson, author of the famous "Anybody's Bike Book," is also a dedicated cyclo-cross racer. As you'll see from his article, Tom's taken a more than glancing look at the requirements of this winter variation of cycle racing.

Cyclo-cross racing, though it has none of the pomp and pageant of road or track racing, can be more challenging than either. If you want to get serious about this kind of race, prepare your bike, your body and your mind for the challenge it will pose for all three.

The bicycle should be carefully picked and equipped. You want a strong, light, resilient frame, one with double-butted high carbon or chrome molybdenum steel tubing. Some heavy duty straight gauge tubes are suitable, but *don't* use an extra-light (time trial or record attempt) frame. A butted fork with the flat-top lugged crown will work better than the plug-and-sloped crown type; the latter will either be too weak or too stiff. Butted-gauge fork blades, especially those with round rather than oval or "D" cross-sections, rise best to the challenges of fallen logs and unexpected boulders.

Frame geometry on cyclo-cross bikes varies widely, depending on the weight, size and riding technique of the rider. As a general rule, though, frames with less critical head and seat tube angles are used (72-74° and 71-73°, respectively). Bottom brackets tend to be quite high (drop of five to six centimeters), and the top tubes are often longer than on road machines of the same size,to keep the handlebars away from the rider's knees. Racers often choose relatively small frames, to facilitate mounting and dismounting. If you are at all versed in frame-talk, you'll have deduced that a bike with a cyclo-cross frame has all the delicacy and sensitive handling of a Caterpillar tractor. Well, what do you expect? Ever hear of a Maserati that won the Baja 1000?

If you can't afford a custom cyclo-cross frame, it might be some comfort to you to know that many older all-purpose frames, especially those made with butted forks, will work quite passably, and will probably outlast the bike's wheels by far.

Get wheels that are as strong as possible, with that in mind. One combination of parts that seems to work well is a Phil Wood hub with Union heavy-duty

(15 gauge) spokes, laced up three or four cross to a Fiamme red label or a Weinman No. 293 ferruled rim. Some people like the Super Champion rim. I've found it a little less durable. Others like the Campy low flange hubs, but they require frequent overhauls.

Whatever rim and hub you use, spoke and true the wheel relatively tight. It may be worth it to have a real ace wheelbuilder do the final truing and tightening; for some mystic (or maybe not so mystic) reason, the wheels I tighten up myself never last as long as the ones I have finished by a pro. After you have had to shell out a bunch of dough and wait a week or two for the hotshot to tighten up your wheel, remember how much you have put into it, and concentrate, every time you approach a rocky stream bed, on lifting that front wheel first, then putting your weight down on it as it goes over a rock, so that neither wheel hits too hard. You'll save a lot of bread and wheel-truing that way.

As for tires, any sturdy sew-up will do for the front wheel, but those with rubber covered side-walls, like the Soyo 70, the Barum Protector, and the Clement Elvezia heavy duty model hold up best through patches of sharp rocks. For the rear wheel, a sculpted cyclo-cross tire is definitely recommended. The Clement Campestre or Grifo, or the Barum Full-Cross tires, with their tractor-tire profiles, work best, but there are others that might be easier for you to get from a local shop. These tires are not meant for riding on the pavement, by the way—cornering on hard surfaces tears the nubs off the casing.

Take a spare and a pump on all training rides; to keep the pump out of your way, attach it to the down tube or (if there is enough clearance, as there often is on long cyclo-cross frames) behind the seat tube.

Brakes are a problem on a cyclo-cross bike. Special Mafac Cantilever center-pull brakes, with fulcrums brazed to the frame, are found on many European Cross bikes, and they are far and away the best, but if you can't find the brakes and someone who can do a first-rate job of brazing them to your frame here in the States, a simpler solution is to get good side-pull brakes, which will give fairly good braking power, and still move far enough away from the rim when released so that mud and grass don't collect on the shoes. Normal center-pull brakes, with their short brake shoe travel, clog with mud. Campagnolo or Shimano side-pulls are great, but costly. The Universal, Weinmann, and Dia-Compe side-pull models are quite useable, and much cheaper.

A wide range of gears is necessary for cyclo-cross riding. Use 42-tooth and 52-tooth chainwheels, or some range at least that wide, and a smooth progression of sprockets on the freewheel like 14-17-20-24-28 or 14-17-21-25-30. To handle the wide range of chain length, use either the Sun Tour VT or the Simplex Criterium derailleur. The Campy, Shimano, and Sun Tour front changers all work fine, but if you don't want to have all those parts down there to foul with mud or get broken in the scramble, you can either learn to use your fingers to switch the chain from one chainwheel to the other (which is a hairy trick when dodging obstacles), or you can just make do with one chainwheel, like a 42- or 44-tooth one. Special chain guide rings are made by Campy, Sugino, and Shimano that can be mounted on either side of the single chainwheel, making a slot that the chain can't jump out of. You just have to get used to the loss of your highest gear, which you might miss on a fast course. Take your pick; put up with chain throwing, or get used to spinning a bit at higher speeds.

The chronic problem of chain throwing can be partially alleviated on a 10-speed, I feel, by using a fairly new, unstretched chain, and shortening it to the minimum length for your gear range. Chains with wide sideplates (measured in the vertical plane) like the Sedis tend to stay on better than the lighter, more durable but skinnier Regina chains. An excellent compromise between the two, I've found, is the Diamond chain, a US product. It will outlast any other chain I've seen, and has fairly wide side-plates. Just make sure your chainwheels and sprockets are unworn when you put on a new Diamond chain; they are very unforgiving.

If, after trying all the above solutions to the chain-throwing problem, you still find yourself spending more time pulling your chain out of the mud than riding with it on the bike, there is one drastic, final solution: convert your cyclo-cross bike to a three-speed. Don't laugh. The three gears obtained with a Sturmey-Archer SW hub, a 39-tooth chainwheel, and an 18-tooth sprocket, are 45.2 inches, 54.2 inches, and 75.8 inches. The range is wide enough for any course but one that has a fast, paved downhill. The in-between gears are missed, and for most racers, the range is a bit limited, but what won me over was the fact that although the system weighs no more than the derailleur and longer chain, it protects the changer from falls and the destructive effects of sticks getting stuck through the chain and into the spokes; on derailleur systems, this causes the changer to be wrapped around the back wheel, breaking it off or bending it beyond repair. I'd rather work a little harder, and spend a little less on mangled hardware.

Use wide handlebars, with a shallow drop if possible, and good, sturdy handlebar-tip gear levers, like the Sun Tour ones. The wider the bars, the better your balance and control will be at slow speeds. Some racers like to raise the stem so the bars are high and their weight is shifted toward the back wheel for traction; others lower the seat for the same purpose, and to facilitate mounting and dismounting. Both position alterations make for less efficient pedalling, it seems to me. The type of seat, on the other hand, can contribute to good control. If you are flying down a switchback trail, more or less by the seat of your pants and half out of control, it's nice to know that the seat of your pants will stay on the seat of the bike. Suede-covered nylon seats, with their rough surface, keep you in place much better than the smoother leather or plastic seats, even when riding in the rain.

As for clothes, wear tights, shorts and long socks to keep thorn and poison oak/ivy problems to a minimum. Wear a helmet in case you hit something larger and more solid, like a tree trunk.

It's nice to wear a couple of old sweatshirts for the first couple of weeks of training, so there's a little padding on your shoulders where you rest the top tube of the frame while carrying. To make sure that nothing cuts into your padding or your shoulder, use brazed-on cable housing stops on *top* of the top tube for the rear brake cable. If you can't get those, use a screw-on stop near the front end of the tube, then fix your seat post permanently at the level you want and drill a hole through it just above the seat lug of the frame. This hole should be just big enough for a cable housing; a three-inch piece of housing is enough to take the cable through the curve and aim it down toward the brake mechanism.

Shoes. Ach. Shoes. You can use track shoes, but then how to you get the spikes into the toe clips? Or you can use cycling shoes, but then how do you run up slippery embankments? There are no perfect solutions, only compromises. Cyclo-cross cleats are made by T.A., and you can nail or bolt them to most cycling shoes. They have one-inch spikes set behind the pedal slots, and are known as "Spider Man" cleats. The spikes are removeable so the cleats can be used more conveniently during the dry seasons. If you find the TA cleats too flimsy (mine kept breaking in half at the slot and flapping all over the place), you can use soccer shoes and file the toe-cleats down, or use cleatless jogging shoes and file a shallow slot for the pedals right into the rubber sole, or you can use winter cycling boots, as one economical bloke did, and glue pieces of welcome mat to the toes and screw old golf cleats into the heels; he clipped all the rubber nubs on the welcome mat down to about 1/8 inch, so they gave some traction without collecting mud.

Whichever compromise you work out for shoes, you'll find that you have difficulty getting them in and out of the toe-clips. In the confusion, the toe-clips often get mashed flat or broken off or snagged on the bround and bent into weird shapes. Why use them at all? Good question. In high speed descents or level ground pedalling, you want your feet to stay firmly on the pedals; if your shoes and the pedals are both wet and slippery, things tend to go awry. So use toe-clips, but adapt them to the purpose. First, use extra-wide pedals, like the Lyotard No. 240 Course ones, or something comparable. Then take two pairs of toe-clips and put a pair on each pedal. Take the metal end-loop for the strap off the inside clip, and rivet the two clips together. It's a hassle, but once you've done it the clips will last for years, and you'll be able to get in and out of them much easier.

So. Your bike is all set. Now for the real chore, getting the old bod in shape. You want to get in shape the way the Belgians and West Germans do? Try running. Lost and lots and lots and lots of it. Cycling is o.k. too, but there's nothing like lots and lots and lots of running. Like several miles in the soft sand down at the beach (not on that hard-packed strip at the water's edge, brudder, I mean up on the dry, soft, uneven stuff you can hardly walk through) for a period of six months or so. Or 10-15 miles a day of rapid jogging on cinders for the same six months. A slow, endless aerobic program, if you see what I mean. And then, as the season approaches, start doing some wind-sprints. In the soft sand. Carrying your bike.

Practice for ½-hour every day at the art of leaping off the bike, snatching it up to your shoulder, hopping over a log, putting the bike down, hopping onto it, and getting your toes back into the clips, until you can do the whole move without slowing your forward motion one iota.

Then start working on the Stairs. The Stairs? No, God, no, not the Stairs. Yes. The Stairs. Jog up and down a flight of 50 or so twice each day, as a starter, then try, over a period of several weeks, to work up to 10 times up and down the 50 stairs, carrying the bike, and sprinting alternately in both directions. That'll get you almost ready to go out on your first European Cyclo-cross race, if you have any interest left in the sport.

For those of you (and I'm with you) who don't want to get quite as serious as the Europeans, you can try training simply by doing the sport. Lots more fun. And it gets you in shape, somewhat. The problem with that kind of training, though, is that it often gets you into anaerobic exertion, better known as the cussing and gasping-for-air stage, and that, they tell us, can wear the bod down, instead of tuning it up. Oh, well, I don't want to go to Europe in the dead of winter anyway. If you do, because you want to get into some races with the world's best, train the way they do, and good luck!

As for technique, the preparedness of your mind and reflexes, there are many tricks which you can only learn by trying them. Just keep two basic rules in mind. First, keep your momentum up; this means you must always be searching out the best traction available, when there is traction to be had, and then applying lots of beef to the pedals, in a gear that's neither too high nor too low. Second, keep your body motions smooth. This doesn't mean just pedalling, it also applies to mounting, dismounting, cornering, dodging obstacles and braking. Keep them all smooth and you will waste less energy, saving it for those spurts needed in extra rough spots. You'll also stay in better balance, so you're ready for the unexpected.

The greatest joy of the sport is precisely that strange feeling of gravity-defying balance that you can't get on any road or track, but that fills you as you jounce, side-slip and bank through an endless slalom of rocks, branches, mud puddles, sand, and weeds. It's exasperating if each obstacle stops you, but it's delightful when you and your bike dodge or hop over all the pitfalls and bounce on through the wilds like some errant ballet dancer taking his tempo not from music but from the natural obstacle course. The rapid pace of the sport, when done properly, calls forth all the strength and responsiveness that bike and rider can offer. Who needs pomp?